The Migration
of Moro

The
Migration
of
Moro

My Other Grandfather's Story

Roland R. Bianchi

FITHIAN PRESS
SANTA BARBARA 1997

Acknowledgements

A gracious thank-you to Mrs. Helen Haladyna, Mrs. Petey Grant, Mrs. Susan Hearn, and Mr. Bob Chun for their technical, grammatical, and historical assistance. I would especially like to thank my wife, Judy, who put up with me and encouraged these humble efforts.

•

I cannot authenticate all the persons, places, events, and dates because much of this story is based on hearsay derived from interviews with relatives and/or their acquaintances. Any similarities between characters, their names and occupations, and those of people now deceased or presently alive is purely coincidental.

Copyright © 1997 by Roland R. Bianchi
All rights reserved
Printed in the United States of America

Published by Fithian Press
A division of Daniel and Daniel, Publishers, Inc.
Post Office Box 1525
Santa Barbara, CA 93102

LIBRARY OF CONGRESS CATALOGING-IN-PUBLICATION DATA
Bianchi, Roland R., (date)
    The migration of Moro : my other grandfather's story / Roland R.
Bianchi.
        p.   cm.
    ISBN 1-56474-209-1
    1. Campi, Moro.   2. Italian Americans—California—San Francisco—
Biography.   3. Teamsters—California—San Francisco—Biography.
    I. Title.
979.4'6100451'0092—dc21
[B]   97-535
                                                              CIP

Dedication

*To my mother
in gratitude for her collaboration, editorial
influence, and her keen memory that
resurrected the facts and made
this story possible.*

CONTENTS

The Genetic Links

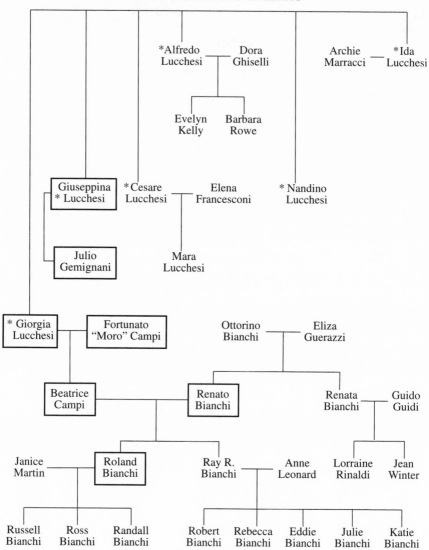

Six of thirteen siblings who came to America; seven others remained in Italy.

Introduction

You know when your own mother is stonewalling you.

"Why is it you don't know very much about them?" I asked.

"I was only in my teens when my mother died," she answered, "and my father died a year later in the flu epidemic. I know they both came from St. Allesio and San Donato, near Lucca. My father was a teamster with my uncle, the husband of my aunt who raised me.... That's all I know."

That's all I ever knew while growing up. When my own children asked me about my mother's parents, the foregoing was all I could repeat to them.

The explanation seemed so incomplete and inadequate. When I persisted, asking my mother some hard questions about Moro and Giorgia Campi, I'd get a cold "I wouldn't know about that." And that was that.

My three boys used to remark, "You're always talking about Nonno, your paternal grandfather, and what he did. How is it you know practically nothing about your mom's folks?"

I sympathized with my boys and felt that they were entitled to know more about their great-grandparents, the Campis, so I resolved to try an "end run" around my mom's terse responses.

My investigation began with yet another leading question to my mom.

"Can you name your mother's brothers and sisters? I know your dad, Moro, had only one brother, who went to South America."*

"I don't know if I can," Mom said pensively. "There were thirteen brothers and sisters in the Lucchesi family. My mom, Giorgia, of course, and Giuseppina, her older sister, who raised me. Then there were some boys, my uncles Alfred, Cesare and Nandino. Another sister, Zia Ida...."

"That's six," I interrupted, counting my exposed fingers. "What about the other seven?"

"Never knew them," said my mom. "They stayed in Italy and died there."

"So, you must have cousins in Italy?" I speculated.

"I guess so," responded mom. I was beginning to detect that glazed look that told me I wasn't about to learn much more.

It wasn't much to go on, but I figured the geometric progression from thirteen siblings and their offspring would be a source of information I could tap or explore. Some distant cousin, at least as curi-

---

*Moro was to have accompanied his younger brother, Emilio Campi, who emigrated and raised a family in Brazil. A serious dog bite from a pet on the day before they were to leave almost cost Moro the loss of his eye. Recuperation delayed his plans to accompany his brother, and medical costs depleted his funds earmarked for his travel. This delay influenced his joining his *paisano*, Julio Gemignani, to go to Naples and "hang around the docks." Many, many years later, Emilio Campi's family left Brazil at Moro's invitation, and the brothers were reunited in San Francisco. But that's another story...addressed in a later chapter.

ous as I, might be willing to share some family lore or facts that Mom either didn't know or was unwilling to communicate.

What I uncovered is the story of Fortunato Campi, my maternal grandfather, who was called Moro, and his traveling *paisano* companion, Julio Gemignani. They came to America together and to San Francisco in the late 1890s.

It took some gentle "blackmail" for my mom to finally own up to some of the facts she was keeping from me. As we shall see, her motives were forgivable.

1

The Cargo Net

"What he say?"

"The first mate said if anyone tries to jump ship, they have bounty hunters with dogs that will run him down and return him to the ship, dead or alive."

"It's a bluff," said Moro.

"How can you be so sure?" snapped Julio. "I was there when Antonnini said it. Antonnini doesn't lie."

You cannot invent names like Fortunato Campi and Julio Gemignani. They were real young men in their twenties who came to San Francisco at the turn of the century. Like immigrants before them, they imagined that poverty in America was better than poverty in Lucca, Italy. If you worked hard in America, there was a promise of steady meals. In Lucca the men had known hunger.

Fortunato was called Moro because of his dark complexion. He had pitch-black curly hair, a bull neck and chest, and an imposing handlebar mustache, typical of the times. His buddy, Julio, and he had grown up together in the little township of San Donato in Tuscany.

As young adults, Moro and Julio had decided to go to Naples to "hang around the docks." They lived by their wits, loading and unloading ships and keeping a sharp ear for news about voyages destined for America. They weren't interested in the passenger liners because they felt they couldn't qualify as crew members. Crewmen for passenger ships to New York had to be experienced. They were in high demand for the popular Atlantic crossings taking place on such vessels as the *Bretagna* and the *Rex* and others that made up part of the North Atlantic fleet during the great European immigrations at the turn of the century.

A tramp steamer of Italian registry called the *Archimede* had posted notices for apprentice seamen for a trip around the Horn. Its ultimate destination was San Francisco. Moro and Julio weren't too enthusiastic about the notice at first. The tales of ill-fated voyages around South America were legendary; these trips took months, and conditions aboard tramp steamers were harsh. But the advantage was that it was easier to "jump ship" from a merchant vessel than from a passenger liner, where customs and immigration regulations were strictly enforced at Ellis Island.

But eventually the impatience of youth convinced Moro and Julio to chance the long way around. Besides, there was no telling when another ship might sail for America; there were no immediate prospects for a merchant ship going to New York from Naples. They signed up as apprentice deck hands on the *Archimede*, which meant they got the worst jobs, late watches, and the filthiest accommodations in the crew quarters in the bow beyond the forward hatch.

The trip was miserable and plagued with foul weather from the start. The captain of the *Archimede* was a malcontent and alcoholic given to the old school of tyrannical command. Had it not been for the skills of the first mate, Antonnini, no one would have survived the Strait of Magellan.

Seasoned "old salts" were saying they were just days away from San Francisco. Moro and Julio became anxious because they didn't know how they were going to abandon ship. They didn't dare consult with anyone, nor did they have a plan. They were novices and knew little about port procedures and maritime security. They would have to be opportunists and hope to leave their ship as the chance presented itself. Now, however, the announcement about bounty hunters and the threat of "dead or alive" eroded their confidence; and the drunken reputation of the captain, confirmed during the voyage, convinced the boys it was not beyond his ability to carry out the threat.

When the *Archimede* neared Mile Rock, west of San Francisco, a pilot schooner approached to let on a pilot. The harbor pilot came aboard to steer the tramp steamer through the Golden Gate. The senior sailors on the *Archimede* were pointing southeast to land, saying, "There's San Francisco—lots of good women in 'Frisco."

"All hands belowdecks," bellowed Antonnini. Moro's and Julio's guilt about jumping ship interpreted the command as being directed at them—or at least as a precaution to prevent anyone else's notion of abandoning ship.

The *Archimede* was laden with bales of jute from India (used to manufacture burlap), kegs of Italian olive oil and sacks of Italian long-grain rice. Once the ship had docked, Antonnini began making assignments for unloading the cargo. He assigned Moro and Julio to the forward hold with the jute.

The boys realized that any thoughts they may have entertained about escaping now seemed remote. The crane operator was a drinking buddy of the captain, and he would surely be vigilant if anyone tried to get ashore while unloading. There were American longshoremen on the dock, so in reality no one in the ship's crew had an excuse to leave the ship or be on the dock for any purpose. Moro and Julio didn't know how long the *Archimede* would remain in port to refuel or reload.

"How long will we be tied up, do you suppose?" asked Julio.

"We might have a few days at best," answered Moro. "I asked one of the crewmen, but he didn't know. We don't dare ask Antonnini—he'll get suspicious."

The limp cargo net descended into the musty hold, and Moro and Julio rolled the first eighty-pound bales of jute to its center. They signaled the crane operator, and the cargo was lifted up and out of sight and swung to the dock.

Moro estimated it would take ten to twelve loads to empty the forward hold. On the second hoist, a bale snagged on the hatch cover. Moro had to climb on deck to dislodge it. This gave him the opportunity to see the dock and the space on the pier reserved for the bales of jute. On the pretext of preventing further snags, Moro jumped onto the deck hatch with each subsequent hoist so he could see how the bales were being unloaded and stacked in rows about six feet high.

The hold was about half empty when Moro whispered to Julio, "We've got to escape with the bales."

"You're crazy," said Julio, "they'll see us."

"Not if you do what I tell you," snapped Moro. "On the next load, I'll surround you with the bales. They're setting them down in rows. When the net hits the dock, you'll be out of sight. Pretend to be counting the bales and wait for me on the next load."

In the darkness of the ship's hold, Julio crouched in the center of the cargo net. Moro piled jute bales around him and jumped to the hatch, as he had been doing. The crane operator hoisted the load beyond the rows already unloaded and stacked, as Moro expected. Moro breathed a sigh of relief when he saw the empty cargo net return. Julio had landed. Now it was his turn.

"Moro!" came a shout from the crane operator. "I've got to take a piss. Have the next load ready. I'll be right back."

"Okay. It'll be the last load," yelled Moro.

Moro worked feverishly to surround himself with the remaining bales of jute. When the crane operator returned to the controls of the winch, Moro hollered from the bowels of the ship, "Take it away!"

As the cargo net was lowered toward the pier, Moro could see Julio kneeling next to the last row of jute bales. When the net hit the pier beyond the last row of jute, Julio came out of hiding to help Moro out. Other workers on the pier paid little attention to them as both men pretended to count the bales as if they had been commanded to do so by the crane operator. The longshoremen stacking the bales could see the boys counting, but the crane operator aboard the ship could not. Besides, he was now re-directing his boom to the next hatch and seemed no longer concerned with his jute loaders, Moro and Julio.

The boys figured they must act quickly before they were missed. Shielded from the ship by the stacks of jute bales, Moro and Julio entered the nearby pier building and, luckily, their attire matched the clothing worn by other workmen, so they didn't stand out. With sleeves rolled up, carrying no coats or sea bags, they headed out of the building and toward the Embarcadero, blending with the sea of dockworkers on the street.

Moro spotted a livery stable across the road and figured the smell of manure would confuse any dogs if bounty hunters began searching for them.

"Quick! In here!" Moro directed Julio. They hid behind some hay bales, obviously the feed supply for the horses boarded there.

From this hiding place, Moro and Julio could still see the smokestack of the *Archimede*, which was unnerving, but they didn't dare try to get farther away in daylight. With luck, they might not be missed until dinnertime. Then they would try to distance themselves from the waterfront under the cover of darkness.

Their nerves had to be at the breaking point, and each knew the other's heart was throbbing in his throat.

2

But for the Grace of Giorgi

Dusk began to shadow the Embarcadero. The boys could see wagon teams returning to their stalls in the barn. At the far end of the barn, a kerosene lamp illuminated what appeared to be a kitchen. Food smells wafted from it, but were overcome by the pungent smell of fresh horse manure and urine.

"What will we do if they find us?" asked Julio.

"We'll have to run for it," said Moro, "and if we do, we'll separate. Whatever happens, let's try to meet here at sundown tomorrow. If we stay together, we'll be too obvious. Alone, one of us might get away."

"Think we should separate now?" asked Julio.

"No, this place seems secure. The manure smell should protect us from any dogs, and it looks like we've got an escape route behind this barn. Let's sit it out for now. We'll take turns sleeping tonight. One of us needs to stay awake at all times."

"I agree," said Julio.

Despite their best intentions to spell each other, both men, exhausted by the travails and tensions of the day, fell asleep in the hay bales. They were rudely awakened at dawn by a kick to their feet from a pudgy, bald-headed man wearing a dirty white apron around his protruding belly.

"What are you guys doing here?" Moro and Julio didn't understand, but recoiled from a menacing kitchen cleaver held by their wake-up caller. From

19

the man's appearance, Moro figured that he had to be a cook. He didn't look like Moro's conception of a bounty hunter.

"No spek inglis," stuttered Julio. *"Siamo Italiani."* [We're Italian.]

"Mi ciamo Giorgi," [My name is Giorgi] said the cook in a perfect Toscano dialect.

"You boys in trouble?" he continued in Italian. "Did you come from the *Archimede?*"

"You going to turn us in?" Moro realized he had admitted his guilt by his response. He started inching toward the escape exit in case he decided to bolt. He was secretly signalling Julio to do the same.

"Relax," said Giorgi. "I'm the cook here. You hungry?"

"Si," both men responded in unison, and stopped inching backwards.

"Come with me," said Giorgi, and he led the boys to the kitchen.

Giorgi poured them two cups of coffee and broke several eggs into a blackened pan on a black, greasy wood stove.

"Sit down," he told the men, but they were still spooked and wary and did not fully trust the cook, who may have been trying to gain their confidence so he could collect the bounty.

"You like *mezzina* [salted bacon] with your eggs?" The boys nodded.

"Where are you from?" asked Giorgi as he scrambled the eggs in his black pan.

"We're from Lucca," said Moro. "San Donato," added Julio.

"I could have guessed," said Giorgi. "I'm from Picciorana. You know where that is?"

"Yes," said Moro, as he gulped his coffee, relishing its warmth. Giorgi put down two chipped kitchen platters with the scrambled eggs and *mezzina* and sliced some bread with his cleaver.

The boys began eating in earnest and without speaking after being tossed some bent forks.

"You guys got any money?" asked Giorgi.

"No," both men replied simultaneously after glancing at each other, surprised by the bluntness of the direct question.

"We jumped ship with only the clothes on our backs," said Julio.

"We had to grab the opportunity when the *Archimede* was unloading," added Moro.

"They'll be looking for you, maybe," said Giorgi. "Most likely, they'll hijack two guys from the international settlement to replace you. "Honkytonk places are not far from here."

"How long you been in America?" asked Moro.

"Oh, eight years, maybe," replied Giorgi. "I started out as a cook on the artichoke ranches in Half Moon Bay, south of here. Between meals I had to till the soil with horse teams. Hard work. No free time. Because I knew about drayage horses, I got hired as cook here for the teamsters. Independent operators board their horses and wagons here. For their rent, they can choose one meal a day, either morning or night.

"I prefer life in San Francisco because there is more action. All I have to do is cook and occasionally curry a horse or two and clean stables. Pay's not bad, and I can live here and eat anything I cook. Sundays I'm off."

At this moment a scruffy teamster entered the

kitchen and, after sizing up Moro and Julio, he whined, "What's for breakfast, Cookie? More of those dago greasy eggs? I don't know why we put up with you. Who are these guys?"

"They're *paisani* of mine. They were ranch hands in Half Moon Bay with me. They came here to see me in the big city." Giorgi's wink toward the boys went undetected by the teamster.

"Now, you wouldn't bullshit me, would you, Cookie? They look like ship jumpers to me. You guys speak English?"

Before Moro or Julio could say anything, Giorgi interjected in a menacing tone, "Leave them alone!" He reached for his cleaver to make his point.

The teamster settled down to some toast and coffee without further comment, and then left, leaving a loud silence to be dealt with by the three Italians.

After the teamster was out of earshot, Giorgi, cleaning his pans, said, "Steer clear of that guy. He's bad news. He'd turn in his own mother."

Moro said, "Thank you for the breakfast, but I think we better leave." He was worried that the teamster might alert someone on the *Archimede*.

"Where you going to go?" asked Giorgi. "You're better off here. Just lay low until the *Archimede* leaves. What you can do is start cleaning some of the stalls around here for me. Wherever you see horseshit, shovel it out. For that, I'll feed you. If anybody asks, tell them you are working for me. Don't volunteer any information to anybody, especially the guy who just left. His name is Pat, and he's an Irish drunk."

"What if he turns us in to the bounty hunters?"

asked Julio.

"Never heard of bounty hunters," said Giorgi reassuringly. "Besides, if that drunk tries anything, he knows I'll cut his balls off." He punctuated his comment by burying the tip of his cleaver in a nearby chopping block.

"Tell you what," continued Giorgi, "you guys start on stall number three. It's the one Pat rents. If you do a good job cleaning it, plus maybe throw in a bottle of booze, you will have bought him off and he won't give you no trouble."

Following Giorgi's directions, the boys went to work cleaning Pat's stall. They whitewashed the side walls and replaced boards that had been chewed by the horses. After raking and laying fresh straw on the ground, they completely scoured away moss and algae from a cement drinking trough linked by a pipe to the other troughs in the barn. They even lubricated the pulleys and replaced the lines suspended from the overhead rafters that were used to lift the horse collars. Each morning, the tack, bridles, and collars would be lowered with the pulley rigs to hitch up the teams with dispatch.

This teamster barn prided itself by advertising that its suspended-harness systems were patterned after those of the San Francisco Fire Department. When firebells rang for the fire wagons in those days, horses were trained to walk into their suspended horse collars for a quick getaway.

When Pat saw his now antiseptic stall that night, he couldn't believe his eyes.

"Hey, Cookie, who's buttering me up? I know you couldn't do this good a job if you tried."

"My friends, the dago boys, did it," said Giorgi.

You could detect a bit of pride in Giorgi's voice.

"Nice going, lads," said Pat in a sincere tone. Moro and Julio looked at Giorgi because they couldn't understand the compliment. But they knew Pat was grateful when he reached into his pocket and flipped a fifty-cent piece in Moro's direction.

"You boys split that," said Pat. Giorgi translated.

"I can't believe America," said Julio to Moro. "We're making money already!"

Pat's refurbished stall became the envy of the other teamsters in the barn and the object of their curiosity. Giorgi, who hated manual work other than cooking, began to agent the dago boys' cleaning services for a dollar per stall. He kept fifty cents for "entrepreneuring and technical advice." Moro and Julio ate free and shared their fifty cents of the split. Sometimes they even received direct tips from the teamsters.

As Moro and Julio got to know the renters, side deals were contracted to grease wagons, repair tack, or schedule extra oat feedings for pregnant mares.

About a week had passed when the smokestack of the *Archimede* could be seen backing out from its moorings. Moro and Julio had not ventured out of the barn since they jumped ship. The worry about bounty hunters faded as Giorgi assured the boys this threat was a bluff, just as Moro had suspected. The "dago" boys felt confident they could venture outside the barn for the first time to investigate their surroundings.

Both men had relied on rumors that a contingency of Lucchesi already in San Francisco offered some semblance of a support group for new arrivals to America. The rumor was false. San Francisco was a bigger city than they had ever imagined, and finding other Italians (besides Giorgi) to bridge the linguistic and social barriers was difficult.

But optimism was a prerequisite for adapting. Youth, strength, good health, and an appetite for work helped the pair begin as lowly stable hands in many of the other teamster barns along the San Francisco waterfront. Giorgi's delegation of the work he avoided provided Moro and Julio with shelter, a meal a day, and tips from appreciative teamsters. Moro slept on sacks of oats in a feed stall, while Julio found more private space in one of the tack rooms.

In time they became handymen and errand boys for the senior teamsters who boarded their horses and wagons. They gained a reputation as sincere, hardworking "dagos." They appreciated the extra tips from the drivers who wanted their tack guarded, wagons greased, or farrier tools protected. Pilfering was the rule, not the exception, since The Embarcadero was frequented by earthy, rustic men who lived on the edge of subsistence.

3

Teamsters by Default

Shoveling manure was hardly what Moro and Julio had expected to do in America, but it was a start. The only tolerable part of the job for Moro was his love of horses. He had never seen Clydesdales up close, and he never ceased to wonder over the size, strength, and gentleness of these beautiful draft animals. He put up with the smelly part of the job for the pleasure of grooming and feeding the huge beasts, who seemed comforted when he talked to them in Italian. Except for Julio and Giorgi, the horses were the only ones he could talk to outloud without feeling self-conscious. He struggled to learn the names of all the horses in the barn, and these were the first English words he mastered.

A Clydesdale mare named Beverly was his favorite. He called her "Beverlini" while stroking her three thousand pounds with a curry comb or sponging the chafed areas where the horse collar rubbed during the day's hauling.

Beverlini pulled the wagon owned by Pat, the Irishman. According to Giorgi, Pat had won his team of horses and his wagon in a card game.

"He won a prize in Beverlini," thought Moro, but her companion Clydesdale gelding, named Big Tom (Bigge Tommy, to Moro), was *stupido.* Only Beverlini's intelligence and strength compensated for Bigge Tommy's temperament as an obstreperous draft horse. Beverlini sometimes compensated even for her owner, Pat, since the latter drank and gambled his profits away. Many an evening Beverlini led the team home with Pat dead drunk on the wagon seat. Moro and Julio often had to scrounge feed for the horses when Pat's irresponsibility didn't provide for their welfare.

In those days, teamster wagons met the barges full of farm products that came down the Sacramento and San Joaquin rivers to the ferry building and piers on the San Francisco Embarcadero. Grains, fruits, potatoes, and fresh vegetables flowed from the bountiful valleys of the interior. The produce had to be hauled to processors or wholesalers for the San Francisco and Peninsula populace.

One September day, Pat was hauling tomatoes from China Basin to the cannery near Fisherman's Wharf. That night, he failed to return to the barn on time. At first Moro was not alarmed when Julio said, "I wonder why Pat is so late in getting back?" Moro figured Pat had probably stopped for a swig at one of the many watering holes frequented by the teamsters. But as the hour grew late, Moro became anxious about Beverlini and Bigge Tommy being in their harnesses for almost fourteen hours. Tomorrow was another workday that would surely tax the horses if they didn't rest.

Beverlini's familiar neigh and clomping stride broke the night's stillness. The horse's gait and the rattle of the wagon were somehow more intense than usual. As Moro peered out of the barn, he could see the froth on the Clydesdales' chests. They had been running to return to the barn. Pat was slumped in the driver's seat as expected, but this time he was not drunk. This time he was dead!

Before the police arrived, Moro reached down under the driver's seat to see if a chrome-plated .38-caliber Smith and Wesson revolver was still there. He had seen it in the wagon and it appeared not to be functional because of rust and neglect, but Pat used to say that he carried it to scare off hijackers. The revolver had not been removed.

Giorgi and some of the other drivers speculated about foul play because of Pat's lifestyle and questionable friends. The police, however, dismissed the death as due to natural causes. They examined the .38 revolver and replaced it with disinterest. Pat was taken to the morgue on Montgomery Street near the old police station.

Moro tried to soothe the sweating, agitated horses while he unhitched Pat's wagon. Julio watered and fed the famished Beverlini and Bigge Tommy and, after he cooled them off, took the precaution of covering them with their horseblankets.

"What's going to happen to the horses tomorrow?" asked Moro. It was an open-ended question to the assembled drivers. Giorgi translated Moro's question for the benefit of those gathered. Finally, Giorgi summarized their speculations, saying, "Nobody knows."

Moro and Julio worried throughout the evening about what would become of the horses and wagon. These thoughts soon lulled the men into a troubled sleep when they retired.

At dawn the next morning, Moro hitched up Pat's team, just as he had helped him do dozens of times.

"What are you doing?" asked Julio.

"Get on board," replied Moro. "We're going to

China Basin as Pat would have done."

Tomatoes were coming in fast, and Moro figured that Pat's family would appreciate the income that would keep the horses fed. Moro and Julio kept a strict accounting of their trips and of the tonnage of tomatoes hauled, but weeks went by without a word from anybody.

By this silence, Moro and Julio inherited their lifelong profession. It turned out that Pat had no living relatives, and Moro's act and concern to keep the horses working and fed resulted in a declaration by the other teamsters in the barn that the "dago boys" should get the rig by some obscure logic of eminent domain. An informal code among the barn teamsters, which was encouraged by Giorgi, declared that Moro and Julio should be the beneficiaries of Pat's non-existent will. Besides, everyone knew how much Moro loved Beverlini. By now, the Italianized name had stuck and became the household name for the gentle mare.

Giorgi orchestrated a ceremony around the kitchen table, where he had spread out an array of shot glasses and touted the elixir qualities of the bottle of booze that he opened with his teeth. With great ceremony, consisting of straight shots of whiskey and back slapping, Pat's horses and wagon were bequeathed to the "dago boys."

Moro and Julio were touched by this generosity, but even more so because they had been accepted by the other teamsters. They were now responsible businessmen.

In this way, circumstances fulfilled the promise of work in America for Fortunato Campi and Julio Gemignani.

4

The Girls Upstairs

The months that followed were a revelation for Moro and Julio. They learned quickly how most of the drayage income went to feed the horses and pay the rent on the barn. Pat had been in arrears on his rent, and the men doubled up payments to retire the debt. Once they settled into a routine, their frugality and common sense helped eke out a little savings. They were among the first customers of the fledgling Bank of Italy. Giorgi had met A.P. Giannini when the latter was making calls on the owners of truck farms and artichoke acreages in Half Moon Bay. Giannini's background and knowledge of the produce industry that he helped finance made him very popular among the Italian immigrants, who were spurned by the established banking industry.

"Don't keep you money on you or hide it," Giorgi advised Moro and Julio. "Around here, the threat of robbery is high. Amadeo is a good man, and honest. I keep my money in an account with him, and you two should do the same."

Moro and Julio heeded Giorgi's advice, and their savings discipline even provided the luxury of a periodic Sunday visit to the Tosca, on Columbus Avenue, to play *briscola* and *tre-setti*, high-stakes card games. This was the "action" Giorgi had alluded to and which had motivated him to find work in San Francisco. Giorgi introduced Moro and Julio to the Tosca when, on one Sunday off, he had invited the boys to accompany him to North Beach.

An attraction at the Tosca was that on occasion, if there were winning hands, it allowed a visit to the "girls upstairs"—a feature that had not gone undetected by this couple of socially starved novice teamsters.

It was one of these "visits" that dramatically changed the lives of Moro and Julio.

❀ ❀ ❀

Giorgia and Giuseppina Lucchesi were sisters, fifteen and sixteen years of age. Giorgia had gone through school up to the third grade in Lucca. She could read and write and understood numbers. Her older sister, Beppina, had been required to help at home and was therefore illiterate. Their family (two parents and thirteen siblings) had been solicited by a broker who promised free passage to America for anyone in exchange for one year's domestic servitude in a rich man's house. Although hesitant, the parents saw this as an opportunity for their oldest daughters, and possibly also a means for their own subsequent emigration to the land of the free. A neighbor's daughter supposedly had become rich under a similar arrangement. The broker's salesmanship was convincing. What the family didn't know or want to admit to themselves was that the "domestic servitude" in this case meant working upstairs at the Tosca. It was the Tosca management who had engaged the broker.

Back on the Embarcadero in San Francisco, the rumor mill at the Tosca spread the news that some new girls were due in from Lucca. Moro and Julio made sure they were playing *briscola* at the Tosca around the time the girls were expected to arrive.

31

The chief bartender and part-owner of the Tosca was a taciturn Sicilian named Bussola. Julio and Moro didn't trust him, and they were particularly bothered when Bussola invited himself to an empty chair at their card table. Using a Tuscan dialect to ensure that he was understood, he addressed Moro and asked if he could request a favor. Julio looked at Moro with suspicion, and his body language left no doubt he was signaling Moro not to get involved. Bussola didn't wait for an acknowledgement from Moro, but said *sotto voce,* "Look, the two Lucchese girls we brought in have been crying for two days. We've got to calm them down. Since you boys are from their hometown, there will be no charge if you can talk to them and break them in."

With mixed feelings of fear, revulsion, and curiosity, all Moro could say was, "Where are they?"

"Follow me," said Bussola, and the three men went to the back of the bar and up a flight of stairs to a back room.

The frightened sisters froze as the three men, led by Bussola, barged into the room. There was silence and tension until Beppina began to sob. Giorgia's flashing eyes reflected anger and frustration because of the empathy she felt for her distraught sister. Her stance softened a little as she caught Moro's stare. Then, in a pitiful, half-quivering voice, she pleaded, "Please, don't hurt us."

Moro motioned Bussola to leave, and he did. Julio eased into a chair opposite the bed, where the girls sat holding hands. Their only possessions seemed to be the two drawstring sacks they occasionally clutched out of nervousness. Moro was the first to speak. While leaning on the only dresser in the room, he said in his most reassuring voice, using a colloquial Lucchese phrase, "We won't hurt you. What are your names?"

Beppina stopped crying long enough to blurt out, "You're Lucchesi! What district?" Julio answered, "San Donato. My name is Gemignani, and this is my friend, Campi, whom everybody calls Moro."

"I know your house and family," said Beppina, slightly excited. Wiping away a tear, she asked, "Do you have a sister named Pia?"

"She is my youngest sister," said Julio. "How do you know her?"

"We're from St. Allesio."

A rattled and rapid exchange of words broke the tension. Everyone forgot Moro's inquiry, and so he tried again. Looking straight at the younger sister, he repeated, "What's your name?"

"Giorgia," came the reply, "and we don't want to be here. We didn't understand." At this point, with quivering lip, she broke into inconsolable sobbing and buried her face in the bed pillow.

The comforting exchange with Julio had helped Beppina regain some composure, and to try to reassure Giorgia she repeated, "You won't hurt us, will you?"

Moro and Julio were simultaneously overcome by the white knight syndrome and instinctively thought about escape. But they would have to face the wrath of Bussola, whose reputation for violence was common knowledge.

In rapid succession their emotions got caught up in schemes of how to rescue the girls. Julio said he would feel guilty if they didn't help the girls. Moro was fearful of shame or reprisals in Lucca, for the girls would certainly send word back about the encounter. All four talked candidly about the consequences of any escape plan, intermingling their debate with questions about news from Lucca, for which the men were starving.

It was Moro who suddenly silenced the group again by interjecting, "We're running out of time." He quickly broke open the latch on the window leading to an alley. It was a twelve-foot drop to the dirt street.

"Can you read?" Moro asked Giorgia. She nodded with surprise as Moro wrote on a scrap of paper the street names and directions to the teamster horse barn.

"When Battery Street runs into the Embarcadero, look for the signs, there's a livery stable. Go inside to a kitchen and wait, and don't talk to anybody."

Julio was stunned when he realized what Moro was planning.

"Moro," he exclaimed, "do you know what you are doing? Bussola will kill us!"

"No time," barked Moro, "the street is clear. Help me lift the girls out of the window."

The nimble girls straddled the sill and held on to Moro's powerful right arm. Moro didn't even feel the girls' weight under his adrenalin rush. He lowered them one at a time to three feet above the street and then let go.

"Our sacks," pleaded the girls. Julio tossed them out. But he was anticipating a bigger problem. "How do we handle Bussola?"

Moro's mind was racing. If the girls made it to

the barn using his directions, there could be trouble with the other stable hands who couldn't understand Italian and would not know why the girls had been sent. It was Sunday, and Giorgi was off. No one else spoke Italian. Worse still, the girls might somehow communicate what had happened, and it could be passed on to Bussola.

"I've got to follow them," said Moro to a disbelieving Julio.

"You go downstairs, be casual, find Bussola, and tell him I'll be down to talk to him. Then get the hell out."

Before Julio could protest, Moro was hanging from the sill by his fingertips. He dropped to the alley and disappeared.

Julio was in luck. When he asked for Bussola, he was told the latter was busy. Julio left a message saying he would get back to him and, after nonchalantly exiting on Columbus Avenue, he never stopped running until he burst into the barn.

Moro had reheated some leftover broth that Giorgi had left on the stove, and the girls were eagerly drinking it. Julio looked at Moro, and written over both of their wide-eyed faces were expressions that said, "What have we done? What do we do now?"

In the exhilaration of the moment, they began to laugh at their audacity. Even Giorgia and Beppina laughed, but their laughter was interspersed with tears of relief, tears of gratitude, and, finally, tears of fear. They were afraid of the unknown in a horsebarn somewhere light-years from St. Allesio. It was clear to the girls that domestic servitude in a rich man's house was now a shattered dream.

5

Fugitive Lifestyle

The stable's unlocked toilet facilities, intended for men only, was just one of many inconveniences for Giorgia and Beppina. Though the teamsters respected the girls' privacy, household cleanliness and the cooking facilities didn't come up to feminine standards. Giorgi, who had gone to Half Moon Bay that day to visit his old buddies, was livid when he learned what Moro and Julio had done.

"Are you guys crazy? When Bussola finds out about this, he'll come down here and kill us all!"

Moro and Julio knew that the girls could not remain housed in the barn in this awkward arrangement. Giorgi, voicing his displeasure, only made it worse.

"If the word spreads that two young would-be prostitutes are being sheltered here," he screamed, "there's going to be all hell to pay. What's going to happen if suitors start showing up seeking these girls out? To say nothing of the vengeance of Bussola! That ill-tempered bastard is doubtless plotting how to recoup his investment losses because you two nuts abducted his domestic help!"

"Calm down. We'll get 'em out of here," said Moro, but his voice lacked conviction. A quick search for boardinghouse space proved futile, as landlords quickly surmised that two single, unemployed girls could hardly afford housing of any kind. Moro's and Julio's credit was nonexistent. Their brief account history with the Bank of Italy didn't count for much.

The only hope was to talk to Conchita Esperanza, the sorting line supervisor at the cannery. She supervised mostly Spanish-speaking immigrant housewives hired during the peak packing season. She had taken a shine to Moro and Julio while they unloaded whatever produce was being processed. The "dago boys" attempted to exchange pleasantries in Italianized Spanish, and Conchita reciprocated in Spanicized Italian. Though the pronunciations were comical, the language similarities made conversation possible and flirting a bit more rewarding.

Moro and Julio weren't prepared for Conchita's frank solution to the housing dilemma facing the Italian girls. She told them that if Giorgia and Beppina were married, she could then find them jobs on the sorting line at the cannery. Marriage was a prerequisite. If they were employed, she could endorse their ability to pay rent in any of the boarding-houses in North Beach or in the Mission District. Conchita had some political clout because she was the hiring supervisor at the cannery.

The men thanked Conchita, and knew not to ask her for alternative solutions. She had given them her only honest answer, and they knew it.

At the stables, Giorgia and Beppina ingratiated themselves to Giorgi by helping him with his cooking responsibilities and doing dishes and cleanup. Because Giorgi was basically lazy, he delegated more and more chores to the girls, who actually didn't mind helping, because they liked being busy.

The teamster barn soon got the reputation for serving the best meals. Giorgi would direct team-

sters to the many ranches in Half Moon Bay whenever they made a trip to a farm on the coast. His acquaintances on the acreages there would supply
fresh produce, chickens, eggs, and rabbits with
which he and the girls would conjure up tasty Italian
cuisine. Teamsters from the other barns on the
Embarcadero began coming for their meals and were
willing to pay Giorgi for the privilege. His artichoke
fritattas, flavored with leeks, became famous. Apart
from the good food, the real attraction was the
chance for drivers and stable hands alike to fantasize
about basic instincts while viewing the two young
waitresses serving Giorgi's meals. No other barn in
San Francisco had female help.

Giorgia and Beppina weren't affected by the attention of the admiring diners. They didn't forget
their loyalty to Moro and Julio. Everyone knew they
were Moro's and Julio's girls. Flirtatious attempts, if
any, were squelched by Giorgi's disapproving stare or
the baring of his cleaver.

The girls adapted to barn living. They tried to
free Moro and Julio from lighter errands, permitting
the boys more time for hauling. The men appreciated the home cooking that awaited them at the end
of their long days. Because the girls had endeared
themselves to Giorgi by helping him prepare savory
meals for the stable hands, they earned the right to
use the kitchen and its utensils to prepare Moro's
and Julio's favorite dishes.

Everyone, including the ladies, learned how to
keep their distance and be pleasant under pressure.
The macho men knew not to fool around with the
female help, for they didn't forget that Moro had inherited that .38 Smith and Wesson. Moro had given

the handgun to a Genovese whose son was on the police force. The policeman was a self-taught gunsmith who promised to repair the weapon and test it for reliability. Moro had the gun serviced because of his concern about Bussola and the inevitable day they were bound to meet. Moro did not cope well with this gnawing agony, and he felt responsible for having dragged Julio and the girls into what he considered a fugitive lifestyle. The girls feared leaving the barn. Moro and Julio worried too about the wrath of Bussola. They hadn't been back to play cards since the rescue.

Weeks went by and the girls occupied themselves doing more barn chores and using their sewing talents to repair harnesses and bridles for the teams. They acquired more space on their side of the tack room, where Julio had formerly been sleeping, and managed a little privacy by partitioning off a sleeping area with a horseblanket.

Early one evening a waitress from the Tosca came to the barn asking to see the Lucchesi girls. Beppina panicked, but Giorgia came out of the tack room brandishing a blacksmith's hammer. The precaution wasn't necessary. The waitress handed her an envelope and said she had intercepted it in Bussola's mail.

"I thought it was important," she said. The letter was postmarked Lucca, and addressed to Giorgia and Beppina in care of the Tosca.

Giorgia thanked the waitress for her alertness and her discretion in not informing Bussola of the girls' present domicile. However, Giorgia concluded that if the waitress knew where they were, so must Bussola. Giorgia and Beppina were aware that Moro and Julio had not been back to the Tosca since that fateful night. The news of their whereabouts must have been told by one of the teamsters who ate at Giorgi's kitchen.

The letter contained a surprise. Sealed within was a smaller envelope containing large denominations of Italian *lire*. The essence of the message was that the money was passage for Giorgia and Beppina to come home. The family was remorseful over what had occurred. The letter went on to explain how the broker had duped other residents in Lucca. He had been indicted by the authorities for pocketing bribes, and the local magistrate had invited those wronged to testify and petition for remuneration. Although the Lucchesi family had not lost cash, the magistrate awarded them a stipend from the confiscation of the broker's money.

It was these *lire* that Giorgia eagerly counted. They fell short of a passage back to Italy by about twenty-five percent.

Giorgia was grateful that Beppina had not come out to see the delivery of the letter. She knew Beppina would want to return home at all costs if she saw the money. Giorgia, too, was tempted, since the letter rekindled feelings of homesickness. But what about Moro and Julio, who had been so kind and were still risking revenge from Bussola?

Giorgia never mentioned the money to Beppina and pretended the letter contained only news from home. After a few days of soul searching, Giorgia went to Beppina and said, "I have an errand to do. I'm going to see Bussola."

"Why?" exclaimed Beppina in total disbelief.

"Don't worry. I should be back before you hear

40

Beverlini and Bigge Tommy coming home. If I'm not back by then, tell Moro to come to the Tosca."

Giorgia had Beppina repeat the message several times to ensure she understood. Then, ignoring Beppina's advice not to go, she headed for the Tosca with the letter and the *lire* tucked in her blouse.

6

The Payoff

As luck would have it, Moro and Julio came in early that day. Tomato hauling was waning, and these were slack days in the teamster business. Beppina could not tell time. She could only remember her sister's message that she should tell Moro about Giorgia only if Giorgia wasn't back. She thought it might temper her anxiety if she confided the message to Julio. But Julio overreacted.

"Moro!" he yelled, "Giorgia has gone to see Bussola!"

Moro could not understand what had motivated Giorgia to act on her own. "Why did she go?" he angrily asked Beppina.

"She wouldn't tell me," said Beppina. "I pleaded with her not to go, but she went anyway. I'm scared."

Moro knew the moment he had been avoiding had now arrived. He reached behind the wagon seat to retrieve the refurbished Smith and Wesson. With methodic deliberateness, he spun the cylinder, cracked open the barrel and snapped it shut, checked the safety and hammer position, and pocketed the weapon in his coat.

"I'll come with you," said Julio.

"No," retorted Moro, "this is my affair." He patted Julio's shoulder, avoiding eye contact. Then he headed toward Columbus Avenue, past the morgue where the police had taken Pat. He cursed the day he had taken up where Pat left off.

Moro was convinced he was in the most serious trouble of his life. Outloud he rehearsed opening lines that might mollify Bussola. He felt how cold and clammy his hand was against the Smith and Wesson in his pocket.

About a block away from the Tosca, Moro spotted Giorgia exiting the card room. With erect posture, Giorgia swaggered down Columbus toward the corner of Washington, where Moro stood waiting. She had a devilish smile as she handed Moro a folded letter on Tosca stationery. Without losing stride, she said, *"Tieni"* [take this], and then she quoted the famous line from the opera *Pagliacci*: *"La commedia e finita!"* Giorgia showed the letter from Lucca to Moro, explaining to him about the money and how she had negotiated a release from Bussola in return for seventy-five percent of the trip fare that the Tosca had invested in the sisters' trip. She told Bussola that he had better accept the payoff and settle, because she was marrying Moro, and her husband would not tolerate any pending obligations.

Bussola must have been caught in a weak moment, for he was not easily intimidated by anyone, let alone a teenage girl. But Giorgia's bluff, determination, and courage had worked. The release and receipt were in Bussola's handwriting.

Moro smiled in relief and with disbelief after handing back the release to Giorgia. In silence he followed a preening Giorgia all the way back to the barn. He was very proud of her, but not so much that he couldn't be distracted by her provocative walk, which stimulated heart pangs with each sway of her hips. He deliberately lagged behind Giorgia to savor the movements.

There was unrestrained joy at the barn that evening. An ominous cloud had been lifted. It was Moro who blurted out in the presence of all, "When do you think we should get married?" The stunned silence was not long. Julio must have been talking about it with Beppina, for both he and Beppina said, "Why wait?"

It was up to Giorgia now, and she already had alluded to Moro becoming her husband. Jokingly she said, "We can't disappoint Bussola. How about next Sunday?"

Moro and Julio had about forty dollars between them. They spent five dollars of it for two bottles of a local whiskey called Old Kirk, like the one Giorgi kept locked up under the kitchen sink and had opened when the boys in the barn had bequeathed the rig and horses to the "dago boys."

The foursome announced their intentions of marriage to the barn, the horses, and the teamsters, who were their small world of friends. And they made *salute* until one bottle of Old Kirk was gone. Beppina wisely hid the second bottle as Moro and Julio, inebriated with joy, recounted the escape from the Tosca and said how pleased they were to have found two brides from Lucca in the wilds of San Francisco.

St. Peter's and Paul's Catholic Church in North Beach blessed the marriage of Moro to Giorgia and Julio to Beppina in a teary double-wedding ceremony that consumed another five dollars of their earthly wealth. After signing for each other as witnesses on their wedding certificates, the only luxuries they permitted themselves were wedding portraits taken at Sandrino's on Stockton Street. After the pictures, the two couples promenaded around Washington Square in their wedding clothes, greeting their few friends.

Most left the wedding early, for the next day the teamsters had an important strike meeting involving the cannery. Moro and Julio had never been active members of the union, though they knew enough to keep their dues current. The morning of the strike meeting all the teamsters were headed for the cannery.

Moro and Julio loaded their wives onto the wagon, and Beverlini was hitched up alone for this light load and fast trip, not to attend the strike meeting, but to see Conchita Esperanza at the old California Packing Building.

True to her promise, Conchita hired the sisters on the spot, while jokingly asking Moro and Julio to see the marriage licenses to prove that the girls were married.

With the anticipated security of four incomes, Moro and Julio rented a two-bedroom flat on Chestnut Street. By that evening, all their earthly possessions, as well as some cooking utensils donated by Giorgi as wedding gifts, were moved in, and now all four were in a proper house for the first time since leaving Italy.

Fortunato (Moro) Campi and
Giogia Lucchesi Campi, c. 1906

Julio Gemignani and
Giuseppina Lucchesi Gemignani, c. 1906

7

The Big One

It was a morning like most others in the spring, but with a slightly thicker overcast over the Embarcadero. Moro and Julio had already drunk their mugs of coffee in the kitchen of the teamster barn after exchanging pleasantries with Giorgi.

"And how are the ladies?" Giorgi would ask. He never called them "ladies" before Moro and Julio married them. Giorgi found it hard to admit that he missed the women's company, which he had enjoyed when they were his kitchen helpers.

Moro and Julio had arrived a little early this day. In fact, it was still quite dark outside. Julio had hooked a kerosene lamp over Beverlini's stall so the men could harness their team in preparation for that day's hauling.

On the stall partition Moro checked a large calendar where he had scribbled that today's load would be leeks from a truck farm in Colma. The round trip would take all day, so the boys wanted an early start. It was April 10, 1906.

Beverlini was refusing her bridle and bit as Moro tried to harness the team. The horses kept shying sideways and throwing their heads back. Moro couldn't understand this unprecedented behavior. He slapped Beverlini in the underbelly and was almost pinned to the side of the stall for his reprimand. He yelled to Julio, "What's gotten into the horses?" Before Julio could answer, the reason for Beverlini's skittishness became apparent.

The floor of the barn began to heave. The subsequent rumble, added to the noise of creaking timbers, panicked the other horses. Screeching bats, dislodged from the rafters and eaves, announced the worst earthquake in San Francisco's history.

In the confusion that followed, Moro and Julio could only think about returning home to see if Giorgia and Beppina were all right. The magnitude of the quake became obvious when the men drove the horses through the debris in the streets.

"Look at the columns of smoke," said Julio, pointing south. Barking dogs were everywhere, making it hard to control the horses. Fire alarm bells and church bells disturbed the quiet dawn. People rushed out of their houses in their nightclothes, frightened and confused.

Moro and Julio were relieved to find Giorgia and Beppina out in front of the Chestnut Street flat. The girls clambered aboard the wagon. They wondered whether to stay there or leave for safer ground. They pointed out the damage to their flat and to the collapsed foundations of the house.

"We'll be better off near the wharf," said Moro, "in case of fire." Nobody had a better idea, and so the wagon was directed north on Columbus Avenue toward Bay Street. It wasn't long before they encountered a patrol of cavalry soldiers from Fort Mason galloping toward them.

"They're going to declare martial law," said a lieutenant. "We need your wagon at the Presidio. Follow us."

All the words weren't intelligible, but the hand waved by the lieutenant made it clear to Moro that he had better follow as directed.

For the next few days, while San Francisco's bayside and eastern sections burned out of control, Moro and Julio taxied shovels, picks, dynamite, and other supplies to Van Ness Avenue, which was to become the backfire line. Van Ness was the widest north-south street, and it could prevent the relentless fire from jumping west into the residential districts. Quake victims were hauled back to hospital tents in the Presidio, and Giorgia and Beppina helped care for the steady stream of refugees heading through the Presidio and on to encampments in Golden Gate Park.

Three days after the quake, Moro and Julio were delivering explosives to Van Ness. A staging area had been formed at the intersection of Van Ness and Broadway, and while there they noticed the distraught figure of a man in handcuffs, who had been escorted under guard to a temporary military outpost at that intersection. Moro speculated that the man was a looter who had been arrested by the military enforcing martial law. He and Julio ignored the scene and became preoccupied in conversation between themselves about the best way to unload the dynamite. The prisoner heard the exchange, and said in perfect Toscano dialect, "*Scuza* [excuse me], can you help me? I've been arrested trying to find my sister. I've done nothing wrong. My name is Bianchi."

"My name is Moro, and this is my partner, Gemignani. They confiscated our team and wagon to help out in the earthquake emergency. We've been hauling stuff for the army for days."

"When did you get here?" Julio asked the prisoner.

"About a month ago," replied Bianchi. "I've been working on the Mt. Tam funicular. I came today to find my sister, Santina, who lives on Vallejo Street."

"You weren't supposed to be there," said Moro.

"I found that out," said Bianchi. "They shot at me."

"You were lucky," said Moro. "They could have killed you on the spot."

"I've seen it happen," said Julio. "Where are you from? You speak Toscano."

"Bientina," said Bianchi.

"Huh, a Bientinese," said Moro knowingly. "We're from Lucca, been here about a year."

"Hey, Capitano," said Moro to the commander. "Disa man is my *paisano*...he's no a looter. We're from da same part of Italy."

Moro and Julio had built up their credibility by cooperating during the past few days and helping the military haul supplies on their teamster wagon.

The "capitano" (who could have been a sergeant) understood the broken English and wasn't too eager to do the paperwork associated with the arrest. "If you sign for him," said the capitano, "we'll let him go."

"I sign," said Moro. "This is a good man." He winked at Bianchi to give him assurance that the situation would be resolved. The arresting guard removed Bianchi's cuffs, and the latter immediately clasped his hand around Moro's in gratitude.

"*Grazie mille*," said Bianchi. "I apologize if I have imposed."

"No bother, Bianchi," said Moro. "Stay out of trouble, and I hope you find your sister."

The men parted, never to see each other again. But there was a quirk of fate in this encounter. Bianchi, the man they had rescued, would become my paternal grandfather! Two future fathers-in-law had met, never to know that their respective children would someday marry each other! At this time, my dad was still a little boy in Italy waiting to come to America. My mom was just about to be born in San Francisco. As we shall see, her birth defied the odds no less than this chance encounter between my two grandfathers. It was generations later, when my paternal grandfather was telling me about his arrest, that my mother realized that he had met her father and uncle. Nonno Bianchi's account was very vivid. My mom was convinced by his detailed description of her dad and uncle and a "big horse they called 'Beverlini'" that the chance meeting had indeed taken place.

It was weeks before anyone was permitted to re-enter North Beach. Luckily, the Chestnut Street flat, although off its foundation, had been spared the flames. However, the teamster barn had been reduced to ashes. Moro and Julio had to keep the horses hobbled in a designated livestock area, which is now the site of the North Beach playground at Mason and Francisco streets.

It took years to rebuild San Francisco. But the process was a methodical and dedicated example of cooperation in restoring the institutions of daily life.

A.P. Giannini became a hero by his attempts to grant credit to rebuild the city and the Italian businesses in the Produce Market. He set the stage for his Bank of Italy to later become the Bank of America.

A lawyer named McInerny made legal history by establishing the court process to reconfirm titles to real estate properties after the public records were destroyed.

Giorgi survived the quake and decided to return to Half Moon Bay to work on the artichoke farms once again. Needless to say, the "action" that had brought Giorgi to San Francisco had been devastated, along with so many displaced victims and destroyed buildings. But in the wake of this upheaval, and as symbolic as the phoenix rising from the ashes, the sisters from Lucca began to feel stirrings and birth pangs that proclaimed the coming of motherhood.

8

Miracle Birth

Beppina was the first sister to become pregnant. Sadly, however, her twin boys were stillborn. This had a demoralizing effect on Julio, which in turn affected Moro and Giorgia as well, since Giorgia was due to give birth in about three months.

Moro's anxieties and fears about parenthood proved warranted when Giorgia, like her sister, began experiencing labor pains at seven and a half months.

A neighbor, who professed to be a midwife and who had tended to Beppina, was summoned by Moro when Giorgia gave birth to a premature little girl who, according to the midwife weighed an estimated one and a half pounds. The midwife didn't think the baby could live.

"Don't raise your hopes too much, Mr. Campi. My experience tells me this baby is not going to make it. But listen to me carefully."

"Wait," said Moro, "I want my sister-in-law in on this so we both can hear your instructions." The midwife waited until Beppina entered the room, and then she asked, "Do you have a small container or box?"

"Will this empty cigar box do?" asked Moro.

"Yes," said the midwife. "I want you to keep the baby covered in the open cigar box, but place it on the open lid of the oven of the kitchen stove. We want low heat from the oven, which should keep the baby's body temperature from falling and causing shock. Try to keep the warmth steady.

"Now, get an eyedropper and boil it, and then I want you to administer a drop of whiskey in the baby's mouth about once an hour. Do you have some whiskey?"

"Yes," said Beppina, alluding to the hidden bottle of Old Kirk from her engagement.

"I have some whiskey," said Moro. "It's okay."

"If she's asleep," continued the midwife, "wake her up and keep it up until I come back. Do you understand?"

Moro nodded and so did Beppina. Moro pleaded with the midwife to instruct Beppina about what she should do for Giorgia, who was hemorrhaging badly. Before the midwife left, she said, "If the baby is still alive after three days, there's a chance she might survive."

On the third day, Moro was still administering whiskey and tending to Giorgia, who was still very weak from her difficult labor.

As it became apparent that the little baby could suckle and that Giorgia could nurse it, Julio and Beppina made arrangements for the baby's christening for fear that she could die unexpectedly.

The baby was christened Beatrice, after Dante's heroine, on May 8, 1909, by the same priest who had performed the wedding at St. Peter's and Paul's.

Not only did Beatrice survive, but fate decreed that she become my mother. I can't help but ponder, in my reflective moments, about the midwife whose name was lost in obscurity. She undoubtedly saved my mother's life. And how bizarre that I probably owe my being here to the remote chance that there was a cigar box handy when it was needed.

May 8, 1909, is the date we acknowledge when we celebrate my mother's birthday, and it is the date on her baptismal certificate prepared by the church. Beppina, in later years, insisted that no one really kept track of whether Mom was christened three or more than three days after her delivery. She couldn't remember. It was agreed that Beatrice was born somewhere near the day when Moro and Julio decided to sell Bigge Tommy so that they could pay the midwife.

Neither Moro nor Julio liked Bigge Tommy much because of his ornery disposition, but they were concerned about the effect on Beverlini of losing her harness partner. Indeed, Beverlini ate sporadically after the sale and seemed listless for a long time.

Moro gave the remaining proceeds from the sale of the horse to Julio and Beppina to help pay for their own separate housing. He had always been generous to a fault. Except for the fee to the midwife, Moro gave his remaining fifty percent of the equity in the horse to Beppina, over Julio's objections. With little Beatrice growing up, the Chestnut Street flat would become crowded. Besides, Beppina announced she was pregnant again, and therefore separate households would soon be required.

Beppina and Julio were so grateful for Moro's generosity and so relieved by Giorgia's recovery and the survival of Beatrice that they splurged by buying the baby her first present, a pink ceramic bisquehead "Baby Bright Eyes" doll made in Germany. It had real hair and gorgeous clothes. The doll's eyes would close when she was laid back, and then would open when she was held upright.

Giorgia cried when her sister presented the beautifully wrapped doll, and Giorgia kept it in a place of honor next to baby Beatrice's laundry-basket crib.

❀ ❀ ❀

By now the men had become more experienced teamsters. They contracted for lighter loads and prospered with just Beverlini pulling the wagon. The savings on Bigge Tommy's feed bill alone managed to add to the bank account. The sisters took turns tending to Beatrice and were able to keep their jobs by working alternating shifts. They deposited their piecework pay envelopes from the cannery into a common bank account handled by Giorgia.

Giorgia became the family treasurer. She had a frugal eye for stretching a dollar and a proficiency for numbers, which constantly surprised Moro. She devoted her spare time to trying to teach Beppina how to cipher. Because the households would be separating, Giorgia knew Beppina had to become more self-sufficient. Beppina finally learned to make change by counting money on her fingers. But Giuseppina Gemignani was an impossibly long name to write, and Beppina didn't master her signature until late in life.

The years that passed permitted the couples to fall in love with each other more than their frantic beginnings had allowed. Julio had some luck on the stock market, and he finally could afford his own team of horses, which he shared with Moro. Beverlini was spared more and more because she was getting old and tired. She had become a family pet more than a workhorse. One day Moro and Julio turned Beverlini loose in a *paisano*'s pasture on a ranch near Colma, at the foot of San Bruno Mountain. For years, a very sway-backed horse grazed on what is now the intersection of Chestnut Avenue and Hillside Drive in South San Francisco.

On many a Sunday afternoon, Moro took little Beatrice for a picnic to visit Beverlini. They rode the Muni streetcar, which had just extended its tracks to the Colma cemeteries.

With childish glee, Beatrice loved reaching into her toy purse, in which Giorgia had placed some cut-up carrots. She and Moro fed and talked to Beverlini.

One Sunday, the horse could no longer negotiate the slight incline to the fence. By the longing in her eyes Moro knew Beverlini wanted those carrots. But all the coaxing of the father and his daughter could not encourage the horse to move.

Moro took Beatrice by the hand and fought back tears as they headed for the streetcar home. Sure enough, a few days later a postcard confirmed that the truck farmer in Colma had buried Beverlini where he found her.

Moro, Lina, and Giorgia
The only photo of my mother with her
parents, taken the year before Giorgia died

9

Orphaned

In the winter of 1922, an influenza epidemic exacted a high toll of life in San Francisco and throughout California.

Giorgia became seriously ill and, notwithstanding her determined and fighting spirit, the matriarch of the group declined in health. She had become bedridden, and Beppina tended to her needs and cooked for Moro and Beatrice. A doctor's prognosis was not optimistic as Giorgia faded in and out of feverish stupors. During a spell of lucidity, Giorgia clasped Beppina's hand.

"Beppina," said Giorgia, "you must promise me...."

"What?" enquired Beppina with a little bit of apprehension.

"You must promise me to take care of Lina, if something happens."

Giorgia had agreed to the name "Beatrice," which had been Moro's choice when my mom was baptized, but as Beatrice grew up, her mom always called her "Lina," after a childhood playmate she remembered in Italy.

"Nothing is going to happen," Beppina said reassuringly. "Don't talk like that."

"Moro will be helpless if I die," continued Giorgia. "He has me handle all of our affairs and won't know how to take responsibility for Lina. Please, tell me you'll take her in with you. She's still a little girl."

The sisters hugged and cried. The wheezing that Beppina could detect in Giorgia's breathing, as well as her noticeably high fever, told Beppina that Giorgia was getting worse.

A few days later, comforted by a whisper from Beppina that she would take care of Lina, Giorgia sank into another coma, which was to be her last. She died in bed at home on June 3, 1923.

Her death, as Giorgia herself had predicted, dealt Moro an emotional blow from which he never recovered. In his inconsolable state, he too thought it best that his daughter move into Beppina's small apartment.

"It's what Giorgia wanted," Beppina told Moro. "Lina can stay with me."

"*Grazie,*" said Moro as he left the room to conceal his tears and anguish.

Giorgia had accurately predicted Moro's frustration and ineptitude in managing the family's business affairs, which he had always avoided. He rummaged aimlessly through files and documents maintained by Giorgia, not really knowing how to sort out what was important from what was not. Ironically, Moro had been astute (or lucky) in playing the stock market under Julio's advice. These were the heady pre-crash years, when stocks soared, were purchased on margin, and profits and windfalls were the order of the day.

An especially sizable stock split had once permitted Moro to purchase two ladies' gold watches for Giorgia and Beatrice. These were the only gifts my mother remembers him ever buying for them. The local jeweler in North Beach, of a partnership named Castagnetto and Matteucci, had sold Moro a stylish gold Swiss lapel watch on a fleur-de-lis clasp. The watch cover snapped open when the winding knob was depressed, revealing a delicate ivory face with diamond points for the hours. Moro was so taken by the watch that he purchased a smaller-sized complementary version for his daughter, Beatrice.

During the evenings after the funeral, after Moro and Julio came home from work, Beatrice would keep her father company before she returned to Beppina's apartment for the night. Moro would sit and stare blindly, fondling both the gold watches in silence. He would even pick up Beatrice's bisque-head doll and weep with the doll on his lap, mourning the loss of his beloved Giorgia. He cradled the doll, ignoring its crossed eyes, which Beatrice had broken years before as a toddler.

Fascinated by the blinking feature of the doll, Beatrice, in a moment of curiosity, had "poked" at the doll's eyeballs and bent them back on their wire counter-weighted mountings. The eyes still "blinked," but when they were open the doll had a grotesque look, like someone severely handicapped.

The sight of Moro holding a cross-eyed doll said volumes about the depth of his grief.

Beatrice became immersed in the many financial affairs of her father, who truly abdicated the fiscal and household responsibilities he had always delegated to Giorgia. Beppina could not help, because of her illiteracy. Little by little, Beatrice learned to understand issues of stocks and the receipts pertaining to buy and sell orders.

Not long before Giorgia died, Moro had made an

investment with a sharecropper who had taken a chance and planted potatoes and corn on Terminal Island in the delta area. In a convergence of circumstances unprecedented in agriculture, rain, weather, yield, and market conditions and price had resulted in a bonanza of profit for Moro. This induced him to purchase two new wooden-spoked Studebaker touring cars. In those days, if you purchased an auto, the driver's license came with the purchase automatically. My mom claimed her father bought the autos so that he and Julio could use them in their business. But Julio would not hear of it. He objected to automobiles. He thought they were a passing fad and would never replace the teamster wagons in commerce. Moro, on the other hand, was convinced that horses and wagons were on their way out, and he and Julio often argued about the popularity of autos.

Because Julio refused to sign for his driver's license, thinking that Moro's purchases were frivolous and had no place in "teamster" activity, Moro transferred the title to one of the cars to Beatrice. Julio's prejudice against autos became an opportunity for my mom, who, at the age of fifteen, was probably the only female in San Francisco driving her own Studebaker. She would take Moro and her aunt and uncle for rides on Sunday, inevitably ending in Colma, where father and daughter replaced the previous week's flowers on Giorgia's grave.

Giorgia's death marked the beginning of a series of misfortunes. Beppina lost her second set of twins, again by miscarriage at seven months.

Julio was in a freak accident while changing a wagon wheel on his teamster wagon. "Never work on your wagon with the horses hitched," Moro had often lectured. But Julio had ignored the warning, even though he knew it was good common sense. As he attempted to switch a new wheel to a rear axle of his wagon, the horses leaned forward against their collars to rest, and the movement caused the rear of the wagon to crash off its jack and onto Julio's left forearm, pinning him under the rear spring. The blow caused multiple fractures. The bones were never set properly, and Julio's muscles atrophied over a long recuperation period.

After that, Moro handled the lifting and loading chores, while Julio drove the teamster wagon; but it was becoming obvious that Moro was growing resentful of having to do most of the backbreaking work.

Moro's concentration waned, and he seemed adrift, wasting away and brooding more and more over the loss of Giorgia.

Though Beatrice became the light of his life and his only reason for living, that was not enough to mend his broken heart. He withdrew to the point where it worried Beppina and Julio, who spoke openly about it.

"Your father is going to get sick," Beppina told Beatrice. Beatrice tried to demonstrate to her father that she could help him. "See, I can do what Mommy used to do." But Moro only hugged his daughter and never verbalized any encouragement.

Almost a year to the day after Giorgia's death, Moro contracted the flu virus. In a few months, he died. According to my mom, his death was precipitated by his predisposition to give up and by his inability to overcome his severe depression. Beatrice was orphaned as a teenager. She had only Zia [Aunt]

Beppina and Zio [Uncle] Julio to rely on.

By any measure, Moro's short struggle with his "American dream" ranks low on the scale of accomplishments. Yet he dared, in the time he had. And I am the grateful beneficiary of that courage. He dared to escape poverty. He dared to rescue the love of his life, who also found herself a victim of circumstance. He backed into a profession of toil he had never planned for. He strove to provide his child a home and security by risking his earnings to purchase stocks and play the "American game" by the rules.

His legacy? Two gold watches for his loved ones. Two automobiles purchased in an act of desperation in the hope of ensuring his future. And then, of all things, to succumb to a flu virus while still in his physical prime. It's easy to be bitter or to resort to pity. But the truth is that many were less fortunate than Fortunato, an ironic play on words.

Plato reminds us that there is no justice in the pursuit of happiness. He forces us to think how fragile the links are to our past. How long the odds. How perilous the chain of events from which we spring. But in retrospect I am grateful to Moro, the grandfather I never knew, who, undaunted, challenged his fate no less than did the legions of other immigrants to whom we are all indebted.

Moro left an orphan daughter who had only her aunt and uncle as guardians. But for me, and an army of progeny yet to come, that daughter has made all the difference.

10

Tempest Tossed

Though barely seventeen years old, Beatrice had to face some serious choices regarding her father's funeral and his financial affairs.

She drove to Colma to ensure that her father would be buried with her mother at the Italian cemetery. She also learned that her dad had put her name on his bank account; she remembered vaguely that he had had her sign a signature card after her mother died. Hence, she had access to some cash for the burial expenses. Her uncle Julio was helpful in teaching Beatrice about check writing.

Her aunt Beppina, however, never understood money matters and even considered her niece's schooling unimportant. In the aftermath of Moro's death, Beatrice became very upset and disappointed when Beppina insisted that she quit school even though she was about to enter high school.

"You must now shoulder responsibility and help us earn some money," said Beppina. "With Zio's arm so handicapped by his injury, and with me still not feeling well after my miscarriage, you are going to have to get a job. Zio Julio is trying to find another partner to help him with the wagon. He can't do that work alone anymore."

Beatrice was happily attending Francisco Junior High School in North Beach, and even at her tender age she knew that leaving school was not the proper path. But above all, she had been taught by her parents to obey and respect her elders. Her guilt for having to be dependent upon and a burden to Beppina overruled her teacher's protests that she not forfeit her education.

Beppina's well-meaning solution for her adopted niece was that Beatrice take a job with Planters Peanuts, located in what is now the center of the financial district in downtown San Francisco.

Beppina's unfortunate absences from the cannery, due to the domestic turmoil, cost her her job. She was forced to solicit and take in laundry and ironing work from the Italian boarding houses in the neighborhood, with Beatrice acting as interpreter when English was required.

From the time Julio hurt his arm, and after the loss of his second set of twins, it seemed that he and Beppina were falling out of love. Moro's death became the last straw for Julio. He spoke often of not wanting to continue as a teamster without Moro.

Then the ultimate cruelty happened to Julio. Without Moro, his business suffered and failed because his new partner was inexperienced and underbid on hauling jobs contracted with start-up wholesalers who couldn't pay or delayed paying for their drayage services. Julio incurred private debts (possibly from loan sharks, my mother speculates) to gain working capital for the partnership. Soon he realized he could not replay the loans.

Because he could not face Beppina and his niece with his failure, or perhaps because of threats from loan sharks, Julio simply disappeared! He may have returned to Lucca, but Beppina was never able to confirm that rumor.

Beppina was either too overwhelmed or too apathetic, or both, to deal with Julio's abandonment. My mom heard sporadic rumors that Julio had been sighted in the Produce Market, but these observations were never confirmed.

In less than two years, a vibrant, happy, mutually supportive group of five individuals was reduced to one illiterate, ailing, forsaken adult, with the prospect of parenting her seventeen-year-old niece.

Beppina and Bea's total income barely paid the rent, which had not been increased for years by their landlord, a kindly gentleman named Farnoccia, who sympathized with the plight of his tenants. Neither Beppina nor Lina had yet to fully understand the stocks and dividends left by Moro. Money accumulated in the Bank of America margin account, and the mystery was as curious to Beatrice as it was unfathomable to Beppina.

In the years that followed, Beatrice and Beppina developed an affection for and a dependency upon each other that ran deep. Beppina's laundry and ironing was hard work but paid the food bills. My mom finally learned she could quit her job at Planters because the bank explained to her that Moro's stock holdings were growing and accruing dividends, and that she was really better off than she knew.

"In fact," warned a bank officer, "you must probate your dad's estate; you may have already incurred penalties." All of this meant little to a financially naive seventeen-year-old floundering in the waters of inexperience.

Though Beatrice tried to explain to her aunt that matters had to be tended to, Beppina trusted nothing and no one. She was only focused on survival and her promise to her dying sister that she would take care of Lina.

The relationship between aunt and niece was not without conflicts, particularly about old-country values and Beatrice's need for teenage independence. Beatrice was never allowed to date. Any opportunities to attend dances or social functions were thwarted by perceived economic constraints. Though my mom kept demonstrating to Beppina that she could afford clothes for both of them by somehow writing on those blue slips of paper Lina called "checks," Beppina dictated miserly caution and kept a sharp eye on her coins, which she kept in a Mason jar. That was the only form of money management she knew.

My mother became introverted in an environment that did not provide intellectual or social stimulation. Considering her traumatic adolescence, it's a wonder she ever married.

It was purely by chance that she met my father and enjoyed the unusual courtship that ensued.

Beatrice Campi, about eighteen years old,
just before she met Renato

11

"1 + 1 = 2"

Responding to a notice from the Bank of America, Beatrice went to the bank's branch at the corner of Stockton and Green streets for an appointment with the manager, Mr. Raggio.

"Miss Campi, we finally meet," said Mr. Raggio, smiling. "I'm so glad you came. As you must know, your late father was a valued customer with us. He kept a margin account for his purchases and sales of stocks, and he still has time deposits in his name, in addition to the joint account you are using. We must put all these accounts in your name, as the sole surviving heir. Did you father have a will?"

"No," said Beatrice. "My mother, who died a year ago, took care of everything. I don't really understand all my father's banking."

"Well, we can straighten it all out for you," said Mr. Raggio. "Who takes care of you?"

"I live with my aunt," answered Beatrice.

"I'm going to turn you over to one of my employees who knew your father. He's a good man, and hard-working. If you ever have any questions, don't hesitate to come and see me; but I think you will find Ray Bianchi a considerate and capable gentleman."

Mr. Raggio picked up the phone and said, "Send Ray over to my desk, will you?" Moments later a very Italian-looking clerk in his early twenties shook hands with Miss Campi.

"I'm very sorry about your father's death," said Renato Bianchi, an assistant cashier.

"Thank you," replied Beatrice shyly, as she eyed his smile and hair style with its part in the middle. A celluloid collar complemented his smart, three-piece suit. He had a tan complexion that made his beautiful teeth and smile stand out in contrast.

After an exchange of pleasantries and introductions, Beatrice stood up to leave. Ray escorted Miss Campi to the bank entrance and began talking to her in Italian. He said he would call her after he had a chance to familiarize himself with her father's affairs.

"You must call my landlord's phone number; we don't have a phone," said Beatrice.

"Okay. Please take my card," said Renato. "Would you like me to call a taxi for you? By the way, how did you get here?"

"I drove," said Beatrice in a very matter-of-fact tone. And when she got into her Studebaker, which was parked around the corner on Green Street, Renato stood stunned with mouth agape as Beatrice whipped a left turn and disappeared down Columbus Avenue.

"Did you see that?" said Ray to Al Pellegrini, another note clerk who worked the window next to his. "That girl drove herself away in a brand-new touring Studebaker!" It was rare in those days to own a car, let alone see one driven by a young woman who demonstrated she could drive.

"Not bad," said Pellegrini, and he wasn't referring to the car.

"Hello, Miss Campi. This is Ray Bianchi—I mean Renato Bianchi—at the Columbus branch. Everybody calls me Ray, so you can too. You do remember me, do you not? We met last week."

"Yes," said Beatrice, "I remember you." Such formality, she thought to herself.

"Well, good," said Ray a bit nervously. "I've been checking your late father's accounts and especially his stock transactions. Do you have a sister?"

"No, why?"

"Well, who is Lina? Some stock certificates have been issued to Moro and Lina, some to Fortunato and Beatrice, and some to F. Campi and Giorgia."

"I know. It's confusing," said Beatrice. "Beatrice is my proper name, but my mom and aunt have always called me Lina."

"We'll have to declare, by affidavit, that Beatrice and Lina are one and the same."

"What's an affidavit?" asked Beatrice.

"I think I must ask you to come down to the bank again," said Renato. "I'll need your help and signature to straighten this mess out. When can you come?"

"Any time," answered Beatrice.

"What about tomorrow around three, after the bank doors close? I'll let you in."

"I'll be there," said Beatrice.

"You can park in the bank's service area, in the back."

"Thank you," responded a smiling voice that hung up the landlord's phone.

Ray went to Pellegrini after the phone conversation and gloated, "She's coming tomorrow! Wait till you see her car!"

Pellegrini elbowed the next note clerk, who was a cut-up named Louis Figone. "Hey, Figs," said Pellegrini. "Be alert tomorrow at three. Ray's 'customer' is coming and he wants us to make a 'chassis check.'"

"On her car?" asked Figoni.

"Yeah, right," said Pellegrini.

"Knock it off, you guys," said Ray, blushing a little under his radiant smile.

"This kid is loaded," said Ray. "Look at these accounts and stocks! And she has *two* Studebakers. What do you make of that?"

"If I was your age," remarked a third note clerk named Ragusa, "I'd ask that girl for a date!"

"I'd get in trouble with Raggio," said Ray soberly, but it was obvious he had already thought about it.

Everyone in the note department was a little curious as three o'clock approached the next day.

"There she is," yelled Figoni, pointing to the lobby doors. "Right on time. Man, look at that hair!"

Beatrice wore candle curls that reached her shoulders and were wavy raven black. Ray fumbled with his keys at the door, very self-conscious that the entire note department was staring at his back. Even tellers on the commercial side had been alerted to check out "Miss Studebaker" at three o'clock.

In a very businesslike manner, Ray led his client to a spare desk on the platform near Mr. Raggio's desk. He figured the proximity of the boss would cool the wisecracks which he was worried could come from his buddies in the note department.

Mr. Raggio got up from his desk to greet

Beatrice. "Hello, Miss Campi. I see Ray is working with you on changing the account names."

All across his desk, Ray had spread out powers-of-attorney and signature cards and letters of instruction to the bank's stock transfer department.

"Ray has been working hard for you, I can tell you," said Raggio. "He's even sacrificed his lunch hour and worked after hours to put your dad's accounts in order."

"I appreciate everything you've done," said Beatrice.

Mr. Raggio returned to his corner desk, and Ray began methodically explaining the documents before him and the reason for each signature Beatrice was asked to sign. She has such a beautiful handwriting, thought Ray, and he could not keep from staring at her raven curls.

"How's your car running?" asked Ray in an attempt to break the formality of the proceedings.

"I drove my other car today because the one you saw last time is being oiled and greased."

"Oh," said Ray. "I'd like to see your other car. Is it different?"

"Yes, I'll show it to you when we are finished here."

Ray was still very self-conscious because his co-workers, and especially Mr. Raggio, could listen in on the conversation. In an attempt to communicate a personal message to Beatrice, he picked up an ink blotter and penned upon it: "1+1=2." Then he shoved it in front of his "customer."

Beatrice looked at the equation, trying to figure out the message. Then she became abrupt and defensive and said, "Are we through now?"

*Above: Beatrice with her mother, Giorgia,
with the convertible Studebaker*

*Below: Beatrice, at center, with friends
with the touring Studebaker*

"Yes," said Ray a bit sheepishly. While escorting Beatrice out, he apologized in Italian, saying he had not meant any disrespect. Apparently the formula was a Roaring Twenties way of asking a girl for a date. If you were hip to the social mores of the day, you knew that "1+1=2" meant "How about going out, you and me?"

Beatrice remained aloof from the apology but, now speaking in Italian, as though it were a secret tongue unintelligible to the others, she said, "You wanted to see my car, didn't you?"

"Of course," Ray eagerly responded.

Once outside, Beatrice's coolness turned to candor. In a very blunt and forthright way she said, "Thank you for asking me for a date, but I cannot accept. I cannot date anyone. I live with my aunt, Beppina. She is very strict and I am not allowed out of the house without her."

"But you're here now," said Ray.

"Yes, but this is business." And with that she extended a firm handshake that surprised Ray, and all he could remember was the sight of black curls flowing in the slipstream of the Studebaker that sped away.

"Hey," he tried to yell, "I never examined your car!" But Bea never heard him, and she was gone.

12

Flowers and Nuts

In the weeks that followed, the landlord, Farnoccia, complained to Beppina about the many phone calls he was getting from some guy named Bianchi at Bank of America.

"He keeps asking for Beatrice. Who is this guy?"

"Lina has been going to the bank to sign stuff about Moro's accounts. I don't understand why she has to make so many trips. She drives herself there, and I'm worried she is going to hit somebody."

"From what I can tell, Lina is a good driver; but if you want some advice from me," said Farnoccia, "I'd check out this Bianchi character. Something tells me his phone calls aren't all business."

After Beppina confronted Beatrice about the phone calls, Beatrice visited Renato at the bank without an appointment.

"You have to stop calling me," said Beatrice to Ray. "My landlord complained to my aunt."

"So, will it be okay if I come to see you?" asked Ray hopefully.

"No, we can't do that," said Beatrice with a worried look.

Ray was thrilled by her use of the word "we." He dwelled upon the implication of the word. Though the statement was negative, it seemed to imply some alternative, revealing Beatrice's willingness to foster the relationship.

"What if I come to visit your aunt some weekend on the pretext that she has to sign something?"

"My aunt can't read or write. You'd better not come. I have to leave now. My aunt is probably worried that I've been away too long. Goodbye, for now."

Ray walked Beatrice to her car, and subtle hand waving marked a bittersweet parting.

"Shit," said Ray to Pellegrini and Figoni when he returned to his note counter.

"What's your problem?" asked Figoni. "Ol' lover boy get turned down again?"

"No," said Ray. "I think she likes me, but I can't call her at her landlord's phone anymore, and she told me not to visit!"

"You going to let that stop you?" chimed in Pellegrini. "You can always write. Christ, man, faint heart never won fair maiden. I'd just show up."

"I think you're right," said Ray, and on his lunch hour he went to the flower shop next to Valente Marini on Green Street to order a bouquet of flowers for Sunday morning.

Renato's heart was beating a little fast as he rang the doorbell at Beatrice's address around two o'clock Sunday afternoon. Beppina answered the door.

"*Signora Gemignani! Sono Renato Bianchi.* Is Lina home?" He used both English and Italian to cover his bases. Ray detected Beppina's urge to slam the door. Her stern, penetrating gaze spoke defiance at the brash but impeccably dressed figure before her. Possibly because of the initial Italian salutation, she finally said, "*Aspetta*" [wait].

The door closed more gently than Ray had expected, but he waited a long time, admiring his choice of flowers—which, he now realized, he should have presented to Beppina.

A flushed Beatrice opened the door after some minutes.

"I told you not to come," said Beatrice in an anxious tone, but there was no chastisement in her voice.

"I brought these for your aunt," said Ray, holding up the bouquet.

"Please come in," said Beatrice.

After climbing a long interior staircase, Beatrice led Ray to the kitchen. Beppina had since returned to a pile of commercial ironing and was attacking a shirt in silence. Two boarders, middle-aged men, were sitting at the kitchen table. It appeared that they had already finished lunch. One was drinking coffee.

"These are my aunt's boarders," said Beatrice awkwardly. "This is Renato Bianchi from the Bank of America. He has helped me with Moro's affairs. You met my Aunt Beppina already, of course." Just a few silent nods acknowledged Beatrice's introductions.

"*Questi fiori sono per te*" [these flowers are for you], said Renato, extending the bouquet toward Beppina.

"Lina," Beppina commanded in Italian, "get a vase for the flowers and offer Mr. Bianchi a glass of wine or something."

"Would you care for a glass—"

"No, thank you," interrupted Ray, "Not this early." He sat himself at the kitchen table. The silence that followed was even more awkward, as Beppina kept ironing. The boarders knew enough to excuse themselves to leave the kitchen. Both men alluded to their having seen Ray at the bank.

"You look familiar," said one of the boarders called Paganucci. "You work with Mr. Ragusa, don't you?"

"Yes," said Ray.

"I go to Mr. Ragusa all the time," said Paganucci.

"He's been with the bank longer than I have," added Ray in a desperate attempt to start some kind of conversation, but Paganucci left the room. The verbal exchange that followed was embarrassingly stilted.

"I don't live far from here," said Renato.

"Oh, really?" said Beatrice. "Where?"

"On Taylor...."

"Oh."

"He lives on Taylor," said Beatrice to her aunt in Italian.

Beppina just kept on ironing, looking down at the latest shirt she had picked up, and ignoring her niece and her "date."

Suddenly Beppina reached for a bowl of mixed nuts. Placing a metal nutcracker on top of them, she pushed the snacks toward Renato without a word. It must have been her way of showing her appreciation for the flowers.

"These nuts are good," said Renato after cracking and eating an almond.

"Not too imaginative a response," thought Beatrice. But then, she wasn't exactly contributing to great conversation either.

"You never did examine my other car, did you?"

"No," said Renato eagerly, anticipating some

Left to right: Louis Figone, Al Pellegrini, and Renato Bianchi in the note department of the Columbus branch of the Bank of America

privacy with Beatrice.

"*Zia*, can I show Rena...er, Mr. Bianchi the car downstairs?"

"No," came the reply from Beppina, in a voice that left no room for debate. Then Beppina surprised both her charges when she continued, "I think Mr. Bianchi should go now."

Renato pulled out a blank signature card from his coat.

"I'll need you to sign this at your leisure," he told Beatrice. And he repeated the statement in Italian so Beppina could understand. The whole exchange was a sham. The card was a face-saving gesture that he figured he might have to use to justify his visit. On the card he had prewritten "1+1=2" again, so that Beatrice could see it.

81

"I'll get this back to you next week," said Beatrice, and she also repeated the sentence in Italian for Beppina's benefit and to show Ray that she was following his lead. She was delighted that her "guest" gave her a legitimate excuse to return to the bank in the days ahead.

"Goodbye, Mrs. Gemignani," said Renato. "Thank you for the nuts."

Beatrice took Ray by the hand down the long flight of stairs. They didn't tarry at the door for fear Beppina might follow or confront them. But Beatrice was able to smile and in a half-whisper say, "I'll see you next week."

13

The *Elizabeth*

"You must have scared off that Bianchi fella," said Farnoccia to Beppina. "I haven't gotten any more phone calls."

"No, I don't think so," replied Beppina. "Lina's been wearing out the tires on both of her cars with trips to the bank."

"*Eh, e joventu; pazienza*" [It's youth; patience].

Ragusa, Figoni, and Pellegrini were now on a first-name basis with Beatrice. Whenever Beatrice came into the lobby, they'd go find Ray. The note department covered for Ray so that Mr. Raggio wouldn't get suspicious about the frequent rendezvous. But Raggio was no fool.

"You still working on Miss Campi's accounts?" he once asked in passing.

"I think I'm about done," said Ray with a bit of a blush. He always blushed easily. Now it was Ray's turn to warn Beatrice. "We'd better not meet in the bank so often," he told her.

The relationship had progressed to the point where Beppina sort of took Ray's Sunday visits in stride. Her trust in Lina's "friend" grew, though imperceptibly. Ray was allowed to ride to the cemetery in Colma on those Sunday afternoons when Beatrice would make a pilgrimage to her parents' graves. Beppina gave up her passenger seat to him, and sat silently in back, shielded from the draft by the isinglass flaps drawn on each side of the Studebaker's rear seat.

Ray relished these opportunities to watch Beatrice driving next to him. Her skill at double-clutching sometimes hiked her skirts up a little and prompted furtive glances from an appreciative leg man.

"I'm taking my aunt to Ukiah next weekend," said Beatrice to Ray. "She was invited to visit a distant cousin. We won't be able to see each other for a while."

Ray wasn't looking forward to this interruption of his weekend courtship, but while Beatrice was away he took stock of how much he was really falling in love with her.

Ray had dated Joe DiMaggio's sister once. He had entertained romantic notions about Ida Farina, his sister's girlfriend, who lived in the downstairs flat on Taylor. But none of these relationships had been accompanied by the heart pangs he felt for Beatrice Campi.

Ray had already agonized over the prospect that he was going to have to sell his sailboat, the *Elizabeth*, for the cash it would bring. He knew that sooner or later his growing love for Beatrice would affect the lifestyle he enjoyed with the boat. The *Elizabeth* and Beatrice Campi were on a collision course.

❀ ❀ ❀

The *Elizabeth* was a yawl, a type of sailboat that has a smaller second mast and sail behind the steering cockpit, or abaft—that's sailor talk for behind the helm. My father loved his boat. It had been a bribe from his mother for becoming a banker and not a merchant seaman, which he had always wanted to be, and was named after her. He couldn't wait to leave his job at the bank on Saturday afternoons, when the bank closed early. He headed straight for Gaslight Cove, just west of Fort Mason at the San Francisco marina, to ready the *Elizabeth* for Sunday outings to Tiburon or Belvedere or Paradise Cove.

But now, for the first time in the six years that he had owned his boat, his Sunday sailing routine had been disrupted by his visits with Beatrice Campi.

Ray's first mate was Philip Risori, a North Beach contemporary and school friend whose passion for boats and sailing equaled Ray's. Later in his career, Philip became a successful dentist in Palo Alto. The two individuals were as one onboard the *Elizabeth*. They could communicate without talking, and the subtlety of this two-man crew in handling a large, awkward yawl was like poetry in motion. I learned this from one of the regular party-goers who didn't miss a chance to sail on the *Elizabeth* as a guest.

The yawl had been built in Sausalito by its original owner, who eventually sold it to pay his debts. My grandmother, Eliza Bianchi, purchased it for my dad and was fortunate to strike a real bargain. The seller had commissioned the yawl to be lived on, not to sail much. Consequently it was big, roomy, and heavy. Describing the boat as solid would be an understatement.

It was easy to get my dad to talk about his yacht. He would wax nostalgically about how she was built.

"Forty-five feet long at the waterline was a big boat in those days. The clipper bow supported a long

bowsprit and dolphin striker that rarely got wet because the boat was beamy [fourteen feet], and the
hull was so heavy that she barely ever listed or
pitched, even in the heaviest chop. She blasted
through swells rather than riding over them. Her
tug-like qualities made her very stable and seawor-
thy, yet she was sensitive to the helm. Few passengers ever got seasick."

The *Elizabeth* was a San Francisco Bay boat, in
that the windier the weather, the better. Ray and
Philip never worried about hoisting her full comple-
ment of canvas—jib, ginney, spar mainsail, and
spanker abaft. A topgallant, above the mainspar, was
used when Ray and Phil wanted to show off. Rarely
used, but effective for sailing before the wind, was a
square rig you could hoist in front of the mainmast.
It was a solid thirty feet of spruce impeccably varnished. The mast was encircled by the old-fashioned
rings that held the mainsail. The square rig func-
tioned like a spinnaker. Spinnakers were disliked
and called sissy-sails in those days.

When Dad described details about the boat, the
expression on his face would change and his voice
would fill with enthusiasm.

"The hull was planked in oak ninety degrees to
the hardwood ribs." Dad crossed his fingers to demonstrate the point. "Starting from the keel, two
planks were nailed, and then a space was skipped
and then two more planks, and so on to the gun-
wales. Into the intervening empty plank space was
hammered a tapered filler plank. This board was
pounded in place with wooden mallets, which
squeezed the boards above and below it. The plank-
ing became so tight that the hull didn't require

caulking.

"Then the entire outside surface was block-planed by hand so that the inverted hull resembled the construction of a classic mandolin. Mahogany trim and teak deck reflected the pride of shipwrights who built wooden boats in such a classic tradition that you could call it art."

It was futile to try to interrupt or ask a question. Dad was on a roll.

"The hull had a lot of freeboard, and because the main cabin ran a good portion of the deck length, the cabin space below had headroom to spare."

Old snapshots showed a conventional oak oval dining-room table secured to the floor inside. It could seat ten comfortably. Leather-padded, semicircular benches were on each side of the table. Portholes framed in brass lined the length of the cabin on both sides above the main deck, allowing the natural light to reflect upon a cheerful interior. Two charcoal burners mounted on gimbals graced the galley section to the right of the cabin entrance. The bow could sleep four in standard bunks, and a conventional ceramic toilet operated by a lever pump was convenient and private behind a louvered mahogany door. The ceramic lid on the toilet tank had been designed with bronze fixtures to seal the tank and prevent it from splashing.

First-time passengers marveled at how every-thing about the *Elizabeth* was strong. Brass and bronze fittings throughout kept crew and guests polishing constantly. Rigging was a morass of blocks and tackles complicated even more by my dad and his father, whose marine expertise was brought to bear so that one, or at most two men, could hoist and trim the sails and work the sheets and oversized winches that looked like they had come off a clipper ship.

In an attempt to gain stability and balance, the original owner had placed four cast-iron train wheels weighing tons over the ribs in the bilge. He experimented with moving them fore and aft and from side to side, and ultimately poured cement around them to keep them in place and to add more weight.

"That was a mistake," said my dad. "I worried that the dampness of the bilge would eventually rot the timbers and weaken the integrity of the hull. But the bilge stayed very dry. I periodically checked it out and I never uncovered any deterioration."

The seller paid for his mistake. Potential buyers shied away for fear the train wheels would break through the bottom and sink the boat. As a result, the yawl's market value was low. It was what made it so attractive and affordable for my grandmother, who knew a bargain when she saw it.

Needless to say, the *Elizabeth* was not fast. Because of her weight, her auxiliary inboard engine was almost useless. Philip used to say, "It's like trying to turn the *Titanic* with an outboard motor."

Before the wind, however, the *Elizabeth* could fly. Reaching was reasonable enough because the hull refused to list and wouldn't spill wind. But against the wind she had to point at a severe angle, and tacking and forward progress were labored.

Ray and Phil learned the strengths and weaknesses of their ship like you come to know your wife or girlfriend. It's no wonder that boats are feminine in gender, and one's love affair with sailing makes the metaphor understandable.

Ray and Phil even dressed for their roles. They wore white corduroy pants, white short-sleeved billowy shirts without collars, and the latest canvas deck shoes of the day.

Snapshots show my dad wearing a hand-made leather belt edged with tiny metal studs and a big square stainless-steel Santa Claus buckle. All this was topped by a captain's cap with a short bill and tarnished-gold braid. Such a jaunty fashion was patterned after Errol Flynn, the movie star who had become every sport sailor's model. Flynn's escapades on his schooner, the *Zaca*, moored at San Francisco's Saint Francis Yacht Club for many years, influenced the fantasies of the sailing trendsetters. The *Eliza-*

The Elizabeth *under sail with Ray Bianchi*
(at the helm) and Phil Risori (at cabin entrance)
Inset left to right: Ray Bianchi, Phil Risori

89

beth didn't have the girls, the money, or the scandalous reputation, but she did become famous for her Italian cuisine.

14

No More Sailing

Dad entertained his friends and banking associates and their "secretaries" in culinary splendor. Sunday sails to Paradise Cove for picnics or swimming were always followed by *"Il pranzo"* in the main cabin of the *Elizabeth*.

My grandmother's spaghetti feeds and other meals she prepared aboard the *Elizabeth* were to kill for. Polenta and rabbit one week, pasta and *fritattas* the next; but the unique favorite was my grandfather's "continuous fish stew," so called because it took a week to cook.

Nonno Bianchi had a charcoal cast-iron cooking unit mounted on the stern of his commercial fishing boat. It looked like an inverted Liberty Bell on gimbals and weighted for a low center of gravity. Within this was fitted a cooking pot with a vented lid clamped down so its contents could not spill even in the roughest seas. When Nonno caught undersized crab, fish, squid, or shrimp, he would add the morsels to his pot, and he laced the contents with a little olive oil and white wine. The contents steamed slowly at low temperature twenty-four hours a day throughout the week while he was fishing. Daily, he would feast for lunch on the stew ladled over toasted sourdough bread. Sometimes he added vegetables or my grandmother's tomato sauce, which created a *cioppino* or *bouillabaisse*. As early-week fish stock disintegrated away, fresh pieces took their place.

At week's end, he carried the contents home and washed and cleaned his cooking pot, which would be blackened from the continuous charcoal fire. Then the process began again on Monday for another week's round of continuous stew.

When my dad's sailing sojourns called for serving his guests continuous stew, he would ask his father to add more fish than usual during the week before. Subsequently, the cookpot and its contents became the Sunday meal on the *Elizabeth*.

Into special soup dishes, which fit into indentations on the dinner table, was placed a toasted slice of Italian sourdough that was laced with olive oil and salt and pepper and rubbed with a touch of fresh garlic clove. Over the bread was ladled a generous portion of continuous stew and some grated Parmesan cheese. The accolades from the famished guests gained the *Elizabeth* the reputation of having the best meals afloat. A variation of the foregoing: If Nonno forgot to bring home enough fish in his pot, he would pour bean soup over the toast, and the warm meal would hit the spot before the mandolins and violins and guitar accompaniment started. The singing lasted until even after the *Elizabeth* was moored to her buoy back at Gaslight Cove. Hand-cranked Victrolas played Rudee Valley, Helen Kane, and Al Jolson 78s until the last of the merrymakers was rowed ashore on the *Elizabeth's* dory.

Infrequently on early Monday mornings, my dad had to rescue celebrants who were fighting hangovers and had passed out from the combination of red wine and whatever was in their hip flasks. The wine was my Grandfather Bianchi's own homemade "dago" red, and it ran freely from a wooden spigot hammered into the end of a beautifully varnished twenty-five-gallon barrel. Dad insisted that no one ever got rowdy or out of line, but orgies are a relative matter and exaggerated reports of hijinks depended upon whom you talked to.

It wasn't uncommon for some of the bank's head-office hierarchy to find their way as guests onto the *Elizabeth.* Senior vice presidents such as Al Gock, Frank Young, Carl Barbieri, Frank Risso, Romey Moretti, and once even L.M. Giannini, the president, went on "Ray's yacht." Dad said, "Everyone was on their best behavior when L.M. Giannini came on board."

Romey Moretti, a senior vice president in charge of real estate at Bank of America, played the violin. He kept it permanently on board the *Elizabeth* so he could play it when he joined the weekend parties. When my dad finally decided to sell his boat, he called Romey Moretti to return his violin.

"Keep it," said Romey. "It will remind you of all the fun we had."

And it must have been fun, because when, as a youngster, I would hear reminiscing between my dad and his pal Phil Risori, they invariably broke into uncontrolled laughter.

"Remember when so-and-so's girlfriend got drunk and fell overboard?"

"Yeah, and when the boat jibed and the boom swept three passengers into the bay, and...."

Ray regretted selling the *Elizabeth,* realizing that his lifestyle was going to change forever. Beatrice Campi was not the sailing-crowd kind of a girl. If he was going to get serious about Beatrice, the

Elizabeth's *bons vivants* were sailing on borrowed time.

The boat was the only asset Ray owned. He could never consider asking Beatrice to marry him without the cash that the sale of his boat could bring. There was the engagement ring to buy; then furniture; rent for a flat or apartment; and the wedding ceremony itself. It was very obvious to Ray that the *Elizabeth* had to be sold.

On the weekend that Beatrice had taken her aunt to Ukiah, Ray and Phil took the *Elizabeth* out for the last time. It was a somber sail, just the two of them.

"You must really love Beatrice," said Phil when he learned Dad was going to sell the *Elizabeth*.

"I think I do," answered Ray. "Will you be my best man?"

"Sure," said Phil, and the two rowed the dory to shore with heavy hearts after everything was buttoned down tight.

"She was a good boat. We had some good times," said Phil.

"She's still a good boat," said Ray. "I'm going to miss her."

The next day, Monday, Ray was motivated to visit Castagnetto and Matteucci, the North Beach jewelers, just to see what engagement rings were going for those days.

15

The Non-Verbal Proposal

Farnoccia, the landlord, had resigned himself to the fact that his telephone was no longer his to command as long as Beatrice was his tenant. Beatrice was on his phone the minute she got back from Ukiah.

"How was your trip?" asked Ray.

"A disaster," replied Beatrice. "My aunt was helping her cousin in the kitchen and took off her rings to do the dishes. She placed them on the window sill. We don't know if they fell out or into the sink, but she lost them—her wedding band and a small diamond engagement ring my uncle gave her once for her birthday. She is still mad at my uncle for leaving her, but she really liked the rings and the loss has been upsetting to both of us."

"Could someone have picked them up or stolen them?"

"We don't know."

"I feel badly for your aunt," said Ray, trying to sound sympathetic. "Not to change the subject, but may I come to see you Sunday? I've missed you very much."

"I've missed you too," said Beatrice.

When Ray arrived at Beatrice's the following weekend, he proceeded to his chair at the kitchen table and said in Italian, "I'm so sorry, Mrs. Gemignani, that you lost your rings, but maybe your household can find solace with this replacement."

With that comment, Ray reached into his vest pocket and tossed upon the kitchen table a bare, three-quarter carat platinum-setting engagement ring. Though he was still addressing Beppina, he glanced in Beatrice's direction as he said, "This ring is for Lina."

The way my mom remembers it, she ran from the kitchen to cry on the shoulder of Mr. Paganucci, who happened to be in the next room. She was ecstatic about the ring, but fearful about how her aunt would react. Ray's bold move was truly unexpected by either Beatrice or Beppina, but the surprise worked to his advantage.

Paganucci came out comforting a sobbing Beatrice. He said, "Congratulations, Bianchi, you're getting a wonderful girl. And you, Lina, stop crying. This is a good man. Here, take my house key, and you two have our permission to go out alone tonight. Isn't that right, Beppina?"

My dad had never really said the words "Will you marry me?" to Beatrice. And she never really verbalized acceptance of this tossed-ring proposal. Beppina must have assumed the offer and the acceptance had already been given, for she stepped up and gave her niece an affectionate kiss. She picked up the ring, which was still lying on the kitchen table, and handed it back to Ray, saying, *"E bellisimo"* [It's beautiful]. Continuing in Italian, she faced Ray and said, "You be kind to Lina. She's been through a lot, and she hardly knows how to cook."

With that endorsement, my mom and dad went to a movie. It was the first time they had ever been allowed to be alone together. And this was the first time my mom had been alone with a man in her entire life!

I asked Mom what movie they saw. She couldn't remember. "All I did was admire my ring on my finger. I twisted it to catch the sparkle from every angle the entire evening." I felt pretty stupid that I had asked the question.

When Beatrice returned home that evening at a respectable hour, her aunt was waiting up and they talked, as women must, into the wee hours of the morning. They talked about wedding plans and how they would cope with having to be apart. Wasn't it terrible Moro and Giorgia could not be around to witness the nuptials? They cried. And the conversation took on a painful embarrassment for an illiterate aunt who had postponed sharing motherly advice to a naive young lady, just barely nineteen years old and about to face womanhood with trepidation.

Mom told me she spent her wedding night in Sausalito. She had never been there, and it seemed to her like traveling to Europe. She and my dad took a ferry boat to Sausalito en route to Lane's Redwood Flat, a resort north of Garberville, in the Redwood country. They traveled by bus because my dad was too proud to ask Beatrice to use her Studebaker. My dad didn't know how to drive yet.

A cousin of dad's from Eureka, Nini Pellegrini, had agreed to plans orchestrated by my father to drive south to Lane's Redwood Flat and pick up the newlyweds. Nini was a swinger in his day, and he convinced my father that there was only one place to go for a honeymoon, and that it was the new Benbow Inn on the Eel River. This resort catered to the in crowd and was a mecca for honeymooners, vamps, and bootleggers, who drove their convertible

Auburns, Stutz Bearcats, and Duseys.

Mom said, "I thought I was dreaming. None of this could be happening. Daddy was so kind and considerate and so nervous."

"So, did you have a good time on your honeymoon?" I asked my mom.

She paused before answering, and I was embarrassed I might be infringing in an area that was none of my business. But then she answered pragmatically, "Well, it had to have been a good honeymoon. You were born nine months to the day after your father and I checked out of the Benbow Inn!"

Postcard of Lane's Redwood Flat,
where my parents spent part
of their honeymoon

16

The Campi Coincidence

Uncovering my mom's willingness to reveal some family ghosts has been rewarding and a source of personal satisfaction for me in my search to learn about my grandparents.

I think that it has also been therapeutic for my mom to unload and share some emotional baggage which she has been carrying into her twilight years.

There was still one more bizarre stone to be overturned in the story of Moro's migration. I alluded to it in the footnote on page 10, and it manifested itself maybe twenty-five years ago in an unbelievable coincidence which occurred during the time my mom was still keeping secrets from me.

I flash back to early in my own banking career when I was assigned by the Bank of America to its South San Francisco Branch on Grand Avenue. One day I observed a middle-aged lady enter the branch. For a moment I thought it was my mother paying me a visit at my new assignment. Her walk, age, hair style, and the typical Italian black cloth coat—even the pug of my mom's hairdo at the time—looked just like my mom's.

"Is this where I can open a checking account?"

I recovered from my double-take at the resemblance and courteously said, "Yes, how may I help you?"

"I'd like to open a personal checking account—the kind without the service charge, but where you pay for each check."

"Oh, a ten-plan account is what you want. Please be seated at my desk so we can fill out the signature cards." Had I not been looking at the woman, I could have mistaken her voice for my mom's as well.

"Will the account be in your name?"

"Yes," she responded. "My name is Lydia Campi."

"What a coincidence," I said. "You are the first person I have ever met named Campi. It was my mother's maiden name. She was Beatrice Campi."

What happened next could not have been predicted. Lydia Campi leaned back in her chair to get a better look at the nameplate on my desk. Then she stared at me in shock. She remained silent but transfixed, and I felt like I was being x-rayed. Without another word, this lady gathered up the assortment of checks that were to have been her initial deposit. She rose, put her checks in her purse, turned on her heel, and made a swift exit, never to be seen again!

My manager, who had been a witness to my conversation, asked, "Why did that lady leave so abruptly?"

"I don't know," I answered weakly. "I just mentioned that her surname was the same as my mom's."

I couldn't wait to call my mother to repeat what had just transpired.

"Mom," I asked, "do you know if your dad was married before he married your mother?"

"No way. Why do you ask?"

"Does the name Lydia Campi in South City mean anything to you?"

"No. What's this all about?"

"Well, there was a lady at my desk just now who looked enough like you to be your twin. She took off when I told her your maiden name. I think she recognized the name Bianchi somehow, and maybe I'm making more of this than it deserves, but...."

My mom's old, familiar disclaimer echoed in the earpiece of my telephone.

"Well, I wouldn't know anything about that."

I backed off my questioning, not wanting to force any embarrassment on my mom. The thought that filled my imagination was that this woman could have been an illegitimate daughter of Moro's from some unknown earlier indiscretion.

Recently, during the confessions-are-good-for-the-soul interviews between mom and me, I mentioned I had seen an obituary that said Lydia Campi died in South San Francisco, and I reminded mom about my phone call twenty-five years ago. I even contemplated attending the funeral service undercover as part of my own investigations about Moro, just to see what I might spook out. The bank incident had remained a burr under my saddle for two decades.

Some small voice in my conscience said "Let sleeping dogs lie." Another revelation about Moro wasn't going to change anything, and maybe some ill feelings should be left alone.

But I think my mom cast some light on this mystery as well.

17

The South American Connection

The reason Moro was to leave Italy with his younger brother, Emilio (see footnote on page 10), was to seek out their father (my Great-grandfather Campi), who had abandoned them in Italy by running off to Brazil with the sister of Moro's and Emilio's birthmother! In other words, Moro's and Emilio's "aunt" and father scandalized the household after the boys' real mother died. They "escaped" to Brazil to re-marry and have three children of their own (step-siblings to Moro and Emilio).

Economic hardship reached the breaking point for other aunts left to care for Moro and Emilio, and they eventually promoted the idea that the brothers confront their real father in Brazil and live with him. After all, he should have been responsible for their upbringing and welfare.

The day before their departure, Fortunato (Moro) got bit by the dog, and was unable to leave with his younger brother, Emilio.

Moro's plan to sail around the Horn with Julio was really rooted in the hope that the *Archimede* would make landfall in Brazil so that he could jump ship there to join his father and brother. This was not to be, for the *Archimede* sailed all the way around the Horn, nonstop, to San Francisco!

When my mother was eight or nine years old, a boarder in her house by the name of Barsotti took a trip to Brazil to visit his own relatives. He came back with the news that he had found Emilio, Moro's brother, who was living in squalid conditions, with seven children of his own, as a wheelwright and blacksmith.

Correspondence ensued between Moro and his brother. Moro learned that his father was "well-off," but Emilio had been spurned by his father and aunt, who never accepted him.

"Come to America," wrote Moro to his brother, "and bring your family. I'll send you the passage money." It was an expense Moro could ill afford; he had to borrow it to save his brother.

Emilio arrived in San Francisco with three of his children, a live parrot as a gift for my mother, and a man's diamond ring set into a snake band of silver, which had belonged to Moro's and Emilio's father (Great-grandfather Campi).

"He sent you this," said Emilio.

"I don't want it," refused Moro. "Our father didn't want us, ran away from us, and rejected you in Brazil—I'll never wear his ring."

Emilio's wife and his other children remained in Brazil because one of the children had been scalded by an overturned pot of molten lard. The child eventually died from this accident, and the remainder of the family finally came to San Francisco to live in a flat rented and furnished by Moro.

"I'll pay you back," said Emilio, and he signed a personal note to that effect. But the obligation was never repaid, and it became part of my mom's inheritance when her parents died. She was never able to collect it from her surviving cousins, who felt they were not beholden to their father's obligation.

As Beatrice and her many young cousins grew up, it became evident that Emilio could not support his children, and more and more Fortunato had to help educate, clothe, and feed his nieces and nephews. The wedge of resentment hit a climax when one of the nephews stole the famous parental snake diamond ring. At this point Moro had planned to sell it to defray his costs for his brother's family. He turned his nephew in to the authorities in a pique of anger, and the nephew was jailed for the theft. Needless to say, the families hardly ever talked to each other again.

But guess what? Emilio's oldest daughter was called Lydia Campi! Just about my mother's age! I am convinced now, though I may never be able to prove it, that it was my mother's cousin who came to the South City Bank of America to ask me to open her checking account. Her knowledge of the rift and frictions with my mom explains her behavior. Doubtless, she left the bank harboring historical resentments she didn't want to deal with.

The irony of all this is that but for a dog bite in Italy I might never have written this story; or it could have been in Portuguese with a different set of characters.

18

Legacies

I am indebted to my mother's accounts and recollections of Moro's story and of her teenage years. She will be eighty-seven this year, and she's still physically and mentally sharp, all the more remarkable when you stop to consider her premature birth and her beginnings in that cigar box on top of the stove. True, I had to take some liberties in filling conversational voids for the sake of continuity, but most of the dialogue text is verbatim from candid conversations between my mom and me and other family members. I tried to have her authenticate what I had researched on my own.

Mom came around after I almost had to blackmail her by confronting her with my discoveries and stories about my grandparents.

"My boys wanted to know about their Great-grandfather Moro," I confessed to my mother. "And this book is what I'm proposing to pass on, right or wrong, so I'm relying on you to straighten me out if the facts are not right."

I read the first drafts of this book to Mom in installments when I visited her, or on those occasions when we could set apart some private time together. She would play editor and say such things as, "No, that's not right. It didn't happen that way," or "How did you find that out?" She sometimes became incredulous and would say, "Who told you that?" But in general, she confirmed the facts as you have read them.

"Why did you keep some of this family lore from me?" I asked mom.

"I guess I was ashamed," she said honestly. "I was never too proud about my father jumping ship, nor his rescuing my mom and aunt from a house of ill repute. I felt I wanted to protect you from all that. I didn't think you should be burdened with the conflicts that developed with my uncle's family."

"Did Dad know all about these things?" I pressed on.

"Yes," she said, "but I swore him to secrecy, and he respected my feelings until the day he died. It seems kind of silly now, and I'm glad you know the truth, and that your boys will be enriched by knowing about their great-grandparents. You've helped me become more proud of them."

❀ ❀ ❀

I gained insight about Zia Beppina, and about how she raised Mom and what bravery it must have taken for Beppina to carry on.

I remember Zia Beppina when I was a little boy. She impressed me as the kindly grandmother type who patted me on the head and permitted me to crack almonds, probably from the same bowl she had offered to my father when she first met him.

When my dad married my mother, his biggest challenge was to overcome my mom's tendencies to protect Beppina. She made my father promise that Beppina would never be abandoned again in her lifetime, and my dad kept that promise.

Until her death at eighty-five, Beppina continued to wash and iron mens' shirts by hand seven days a week in her tiny third-floor apartment on

Lombard and Columbus streets in North Beach.

As a youngster I recall visiting to deliver my own shirts and those my dad wore to work—the kind with removable Van Huesen collars.

In her apartment there were always hundreds of shirts, which she kept segregated by a color code of her own invention. Her sister Giorgia's lessons in arithmetic barely helped her calculate the charge of ten cents a shirt. Most customers paid her more, realizing the price was so low.

My mother told me how she had figured out that Zia Beppina washed and ironed, by hand, more than 125,000 mens' shirts in the last fifty years of her life! I checked my mother's math to see how she had arrived at the estimate. If anything, the number is conservative, and the volume must stand as a record of the tenacity of the human spirit.

*"Beppina" Gemignani, the surviving aunt
who raised my mother*

Epilogue

In 1955 I announced my engagement to Janice Martin, my late wife and the mother of my children. Friends and family attended a large party for us. Engagement gifts overwhelmed my fiancée and me, and assorted exclamations accompanied the opening of each gift.

Zia Beppina, then eighty years old, walked into the living room carrying a shopping bag. She was followed by my mother, whose eyes were welling up with tears. Zia Beppina pulled out from the bag a quart bottle of whiskey with a faded label that read *Old Kirk*. It was not just *a* bottle of Old Kirk, it was *the* bottle of Old Kirk. The same one she had hidden the night Moro, Julio, Giorgia, and she announced to their friends in the horse barn that they were going to be married.

Those who knew the significance of that bottle began to cry. My fiancée's family and some other guests wondered what a fifty-year-old bottle of whiskey meant. They were told, by those who knew, about the escape from the Tosca and the night the foursome celebrated their engagement plans with the other bottle of Old Kirk. Each storyteller so dramatized the facts that soon there wasn't a dry eye at the party. This was the first time in my life that I had heard the stories of how my maternal grandparents coped when they came to America.

It was argued whether to preserve the bottle or

open it. Beppina decided. She uncorked the quart and poured half-shots into an array of glasses for all to share.

People savored their sips to ensure that there would be enough to go around. We all said *salute* and extolled this elixir worthy of the gods. The praises would have been no less had the contents of the whiskey bottle been acrid or bitter. As it was, the emotion of Beppina's gesture turned a fifty-year-old whiskey into the smoothest drink we ever tasted before or since. Giorgi, the old teamster barn cook, knew his whiskey!

I was particularly flattered, and I wondered why Beppina had chosen the occasion of this engagement to share her fragile possession, which she had protected for so long. She had not offered the bottle at my mother's wedding. In her simple, self-imposed code of Old World myths, she felt that such a prize should go to the first male who would carry on the legacy of her humble beginnings.

And with that emotionally packed explanation, this recipient renewed his love for the memory of grandparents he never knew, and a great aunt whose courage and hardships inspired me to share this bit of personal history for my sons.

On a special shelf in my study sits an empty bottle of Old Kirk. Next to it is an antique Smith and Wesson revolver. Other than some faded photographs and my mom's antique gold watches and her doll, this is the only evidence I can show you that what I have told you is true.

Above: The antique Smith and Wesson revolver
Below: the empty bottle of Old Kirk